The **AA** POCKETGuide

ITALIAN LAKES

Italian Lakes: Regions and Best places to see

 Best places to see 20–41

 Featured sight

 Milan 45–55

Lake Como & the Bergamo Valleys
88–109

Western Lakes 56–87

Eastern Lakes 110–129

Written and updated by Richard Sale

© Automobile Association Developments Limited 2008
First published 2008

ISBN: 978-0-7495-5759-1

Published by AA Publishing, a trading name of Automobile Association Developments
Limited, whose registered office is Fanum House, Basing View, Basingstoke,
Hampshire RG21 4EA. Registered number 1878835.

A CIP catalogue record for this book is available from the British Library

Colour separation: Keenes, Andover
Printed and bound in Italy by Printer Trento S.r.l.

Front cover images: (t) AA/M Jourdan; (b) AA/M Jourdan
Back cover image: AA/C Sawyer

A03604
Maps in this title produced from mapping © MAIRDUMONT / Falk Verlag 2008
with reference to mapping © ISTITUTO GEOGRAFICO DE AGOSTINI S.p.A., NOVARA
2006. Transport map © Communicarta Ltd, UK

About this book

Symbols are used to denote the following categories:

➕ map reference

✉ address or location

☎ telephone number

🕐 opening times

✋ admission charge

🍴 restaurant or café on premises or nearby

Ⓜ nearest underground train station

🚌 nearest bus/tram route

🚉 nearest overground train station

⛴ nearest ferry stop

✈ nearest airport

❓ other practical information

ℹ tourist information office

▶ indicates the page where you will find a fuller description

This book is divided into four sections.

Planning pages 6–19
Before you go; Getting there; Getting around; Being there

Best places to see pages 20–41
The unmissable highlights of any visit to the Italian Lakes

Exploring pages 42–129
The best places to visit around the Italian Lakes, organized by area

Maps pages 133–142
All map references are to the atlas section. For example, Lugano has the reference ➕ 135 C5 – indicating the grid square in which it can be found

Contents

Planning

Before you go

WHEN TO GO

	JAN	FEB	MAR	APR	MAY	JUN	JUL	AUG	SEP	OCT	NOV	DEC
	6°C	7°C	10°C	13°C	18°C	21°C	24°C	23°C	18°C	12°C	10°C	8°C
	43°F	45°F	50°F	55°F	64°F	70°F	75°F	73°F	64°F	55°F	50°F	46°F

High season   Low season

There is no bad time to visit the Italian Lakes. In spring the flowers are a delight while in summer the sun shines all day every day, or so it seems, with the cool waters of the lakes offering a chance to escape the occasionally very hot midday hours. By autumn the very hot days of summer have been replaced by a gentler warmth. Then winter brings snow to the high ridges, though at the lakeside severe cold is a rarity.

WHAT YOU NEED

● Required
○ Suggested
▲ Not required

Some countries require a passport to remain valid for a minimum period (usually at least six months) beyond the date of entry – contact their consulate or embassy or your travel agency for details.

	UK	Germany	USA	Netherlands	Spain
Passport	●	●	●	●	●
Visa (regulations can change – check before making reservations)	▲	▲	▲	▲	▲
Onward or return ticket	▲	▲	▲	▲	▲
Health inoculations	▲	▲	▲	▲	▲
Health documentation (➤ 9, Health Insurance)	●	●	●	●	●
Travel insurance	○	○	○	○	○
Driving licence (national)	●	●	●	●	●
Car insurance certificate (if own car)	●	●	●	●	●
Car registration document (if own car)	●	●	●	●	●

WEBSITES

Lake Orta and west Lake Maggiore:
www.distrettolaghi.it
Milan: www.milanoinfotourist.com

Lake Como: www.lakecomo.com
Varese and east Lake Maggiore:
www.vareselandoftourism.it

North Lake Maggiore:
www.maggiore.ch
Lake Lugano:
www.lugano-tourism.ch
Bergamo:
www.provincia.bergamo.it

Brescia and west Lake Garda:
www.provincia.brescia.it
Verona and east Lake Garda:
www.tourism.verona.it
North Lake Garda:
www.trentino.to/it

TOURIST OFFICES AT HOME
In the UK
Italian State Tourist Board (ENIT)
Offices
1 Princes Street
London, W1R 8AY
☎ 020 7408 1254

In the USA
USA Suite 1565, Rockefeller
Centre,

630 Fifth Avenue
New York, NY 10111
☎ 212/245-4822

Suite 550,
12400 Wilshire Boulevard
Los Angeles
CA 90025
☎ 310/820-1959

HEALTH INSURANCE
EU nationals can get free or reduced rate emergency medical treatment
with the relevant documentation (European Health Insurance Card – EHIC
– for UK nationals) although private medical insurance is strongly
recommended and is essential for all other visitors.
Dental Services The EHIC covers dentistry. However, visitors with their
own dental health insurance should obtain advice from their insurers.
Have a check-up before you go.

TIME DIFFERENCES

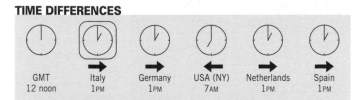

| GMT 12 noon | Italy 1PM | Germany 1PM | USA (NY) 7AM | Netherlands 1PM | Spain 1PM |

Italy is one hour ahead of Greenwich Mean Time (GMT+1), but from late
March to late September daylight saving time (GMT+2) operates.

NATIONAL HOLIDAYS

1 January *New Year's Day,*
6 January *Epiphany*
Mar/Apr *Easter Sunday and Monday*
25 April *Liberation Day*

1 May *Labour Day*
2 June *National Day*
15 August *Assumption Day*
1 November *All Saints' Day*

8 December *Immaculate Conception*
25 and 26 December *Christmas*

WHAT'S ON WHEN

3–5 January *Canto della Stella,* Tignale, Lake Garda, re-enacts the journey of the Magi with a night-time procession accompanied by choirs.

31 January *Boat Festival,* Orta San Giulio, Lake Orta.

February Carnival season. The most famous carnival is at Venice. Within the lakes' area, the best is at Verona (the *Gnoccho Bacchanalia*).

March
Autumn fashion collections, Milan.

Lent
'Hag's Trials', Gargagno and Gardone, Lake Garda. The effigy of an old woman is burned, a sad reminder of medieval life, though the event is now much jollier.

Easter
Processions in the Swiss villages of Lake Lugano often held on both Maundy Thursday and Good Friday.

9–10 April Pageant to commemorate the creation of the Lombard League, Bergamo.

*c***24 June** On the Sunday after St John the Baptist's Day, boats process to Isola Comacina, Lake Como, for an outdoor Mass in the ruined church.

June–July *Shakespeare season*, Verona.

July *Folklore Festival*, Val Cannobina, Lake Maggiore.
Festival of traditional music and dance, Quarna Sopra, Lake Orta.
Jazz Festival, Lugano (first week of the month).
Music Festival, Lugano (last week of the month).
International Sailing Regatta, Gargagno, Lake Garda.
Il Redentore, procession of gondolas and other craft at Venice, held over a weekend.

July–August *Opera season*, Verona, staged open-air in the Roman Arena.
Season of open-air plays at Il Vittoriale, Gardone Riviera, Lake Garda.

Mid-August to mid-September International Music Festival (Settimane Musicali), Stresa, Lake Maggiore. World famous event with top musicians and conductors.

September to mid-October *Music Festival*, Ascona, Lake Maggiore, timed so that some of the players from Stresa can appear again.

Mid-September to October Lake Maggiore villages celebrate a festival of local foods with special menus in the restaurants.

September
Grape Festival, Bardolino, Lake Garda (last weekend of month).
Firework Spectacular, Sirmione, Lake Garda.

October *Spring fashion collections*, Milan.

7 December *First night of the opera season*, Milan.

Getting there

BY AIR

International flights Milan's Linate airport, to the east of the city, is notorious for being fog-bound. That was one reason why a new airport, Malpensa, was built at Somma Lombardo, close to the southern tip of Lake Maggiore. Plans to use Linate for domestic flights only have not to come to fruition although the majority of international flights do land at Malpensa. Malpensa is close to the A26 autostrada which makes its way to the west of Lake Maggiore, at present ending west of Stresa. To the south the A26 links to the A4 offering a quick way to the other lakes. Linate sits on the Milan autostrada ring road, but visitors returning to it for the flight home should note that if travelling south on the ring road the Linate exit is from the left lane (the fast lane) not from the right lane as would be expected. For those not renting a car, both Malpensa and Linate have bus connections to Milan from where trains depart for both sides of Lake Maggiore, but only Como on Lake Como and Desenzano del Garda on Lake Garda.

Some UK low-cost carriers do use Malpensa. They also use Orio al Serio which sits on the A4 south of Bergamo. This is extremely convenient for all the lakes. Low-cost carriers also use Treviso, east of Lake Garda. This is more convenient for Venice than the lakes, but may be useful to some travellers. Linate is about 20 minutes from Milan, Malpensa is about an hour by bus and about 35 minutes by train. Train and bus times to the major lake resorts from Milan are:

Como	Train 1 hour	Bus 1.5 hours
Stresa	Train 1 hour	Bus 1.5 hours
Desenzano	Train 1 hour	Bus 1 hour

Useful contact details and flight information from:

Linate and Malpensa ☎ 02 7485 2200; www.sea-aeroportimilano.it
Orio al Serio ☎ 035 326 323; www.orioaeroporto.it

Domestic flights Italy has an excellent domestic air service operated by Alitalia. Reserve ahead as planes are crowded in the summer season. Full-time students under 26 receive a 25 per cent discount on internal flight fares. For airport information at Malpensa or Linate ☎ 02 74852200. In addition to Malpensa and Linate airports, there are airports at Bergamo (Orta sul Serio) and Verona (Villafranca).

BY TRAIN

Milan is accessible from most major mainland European capitals, including Paris through which there are connections to the UK. Trains from Milan reach destinations on the eastern side of Lake Orta. On Lake Maggiore trains run along the western shore as far north as Baveno, and along the eastern shore to Switzerland. Como city is easily reached by train as is the eastern shore of Lake Como, north from Lecco, however train links to the western shore are poor. Lake Iseo's eastern shore is also accessible by train, but on Lake Grada, only Desenzano and Peschiera have train stations.

The motorail services linking Boulogne and Paris with Milan's Porta Garibaldi station have been cancelled, but those seeking to cut out much of the driving to the Lakes area can still use the French Railways motorail service from Calais to Nice.

BY ROAD

There are long-distance bus services from mainland European capitals to Milan although many routes may not be direct and can therefore be slow. Drivers can reach Lake Maggiore by way of the Aosta valley from France or the Simplon Pass from Switzerland. Lakes Lugano and Como are also accessible from Switzerland. Lake Garda is best approached over the Brenner Pass from Austria.

The A4 autostrada links Turin and Venice, passing close to Milan (the city ring road links with it), Bergamo, Bréscia and the southern tip of Lake Garda. The A8 links the A4 to Varese. The A26 leaves the A8 close to Gallarate (and Malpensa airport) and is handy for getting to Lake Orta and south-western Lake Maggiore. The A9 links the A4 to Como city, continuing into Switzerland to reach Lake Lugano. The A12 links the A4 to the Brenner Pass and is excellent for those driving to Riva del Garda as the lakeside roads can be congested in summer.

Getting around

PUBLIC TRANSPORT

Trains Italy has a good rail system. A 'Travel at Will' pass is available for 8, 15, 21 or 30 days and offers unlimited travel on any train. Reduced rate passes are also available for visitors under 26 and senior citizens. Italy has various classes of train: *Super-Rapido/TEE* offer first-class-only travel, running between the major cities; a supplement is charged and seats must be booked. *Rapido* (fast) trains offer different levels of service and seats do not have to be reserved in advance. *Espresso* (long-distance) are express trains with limited stops. *Diretto* provide a slower service stopping at most stations while *Locale* stop at all stations. In addition to the main system, there are also a few private lines. Two of these link Como and Laveno to Milan.

Buses Passengers on city buses must buy a ticket from bars or machines before starting their journey and validate them on the bus by inserting them into a machine that overprints the date and time. The ticket allows unlimited travel for usually one hour.

Ferries All the lakes have steamer services. Boat passes are available for 1 day, several days, or one or two weeks. Hydrofoils *(aliscafo)* are fast, but do not stop at all villages. The slower boats stop more often but even these boats do not always stop at every village.

TAXIS

Taxis are available at all airports, railway and bus stations and at certain places within large towns and cities.

FARES AND TICKETS

Train tickets are available single *(andata)* or return *(andata e ritorno)*. The trains have first and second classes. Tickets for journeys of up to 250km

(155 miles) can be bought from newspaper kiosks and tobacconists at the station and must be validated by entering them into the time-punch machine on the train. For longer journeys tickets must be bought at the ticket counter and will be valid for the day of travel. A *Carta Verde* offers a 20 per cent discount to those aged 12–26, while a *Carta d'Argento* offers the same discount to over 60s. Non-residents below the age of 26 can obtain a *Trenitalia Pass* which allows unlimited travel during a 2-month period. The Pass is not valid over the Christmas period or for certain other periods.

Tickets for the Milan metro can be bought at station counters, kiosks or at automatic toicket machines. As for shorter train journeys and buses, the ticket must be validated at the machine on board.

DRIVING

- Speed limits on motorways: 130kph (80mph).
- When the road is wet all traffic is restricted to 110kph (68mph).
- Speed limit on dual carriageways: 110kph (68mph); on other roads: 90kph (56mph).
- Speed limit in urban areas: 50kph (31mph).
- Seatbelts are obligatory for drivers and all passengers over the age of 7. Children under 12 years must travel in rear seats and be restrained with an appropriate harness.
- Random breath-testing. Never drive under the influence of alcohol.
- Fuel stations keep shop hours (but may be open later in the evening). Motorway fuel stations also close at night. Very few fuel stations take credit cards except on the autostradas.
- A red warning triangle must be carried and used at a breakdown or accident. Police speedtrap detectors are illegal. Low-beam headlights are compulsory in tunnels. To drive on Swiss motorways you must display a vignette, a tax disc valid for one year, available at border crossings and fuel stations.
- The Touring Club of Italy (TCI), offer a breakdown service ☎ 116. If your car is rented, follow the rental comapny's instructions.

CAR RENTAL

All the major car-rental companies are represented at Italian airports and railway stations and in the major towns and cities.

Being there

TOURIST OFFICES
The main tourist offices are:

Lake Maggiore
Piazza Marconi 16
28838 Stresa
☎ 0323 30150

Via Piero Chiara 1
21016 Luino
☎ 0332 530019

Lake Como
Piazza Cavour 17
22100 Como
☎ 031 269712

Lake Garda
Corso Repubblica 8
25083 Gardone Riviera
☎ 0365 20347

Riviera degli Olivi
Lungolago Regina Adelaide 13
37016 Garda
☎ 045 6270384

Corso Zanardelli 38
25121 Brescia
☎ 030 45052

Milan
Via Marconi 1
20123 Milano
☎ 02 725241

MONEY
The euro (€) is the official currency of Italy. Notes are issued in denominations of 5, 10, 20, 50, 100, 200 and 500 euros; coins in denominations of 1, 2, 5, 10, 20 and 50 cents, and 1 and 2 euros. Traveller's cheques are accepted by most hotels, shops and restaurants in lieu of cash, but the rate of exchange may be less favourable than in banks, which can be found in all towns and most villages.

TIPS/GRATUITIES

Yes ✓ No ✗		
Restaurants (10% usually included)	✓	10%
Cafés/Bars (if service not included)	✓	change
Taxis (10% usually included)	✓	10%
Chambermaids/Porters	✓	€1–2

POSTAL AND INTERNET SERVICES
Post offices are usually open Monday–Friday 8/8:30–1, 3–6 (Saturday 9–12). All towns and many villages now offer internet services, usually in internet cafes. Prices in general are €2–€3 for 30 minutes, but can be as high as €5.

TELEPHONES
Public telephones take both coins and cards (though the latter are now much more common). Phone cards for €2.50, €5 or €15, can be bought from tobacconists, bars and post offices. Some telephones take coins of 10, 20 or 50 cents or €1 or €2.

International dialling codes
From Italy to:
UK: 00 44
Germany: 00 49
USA: 00 1
Netherlands: 00 31

Emergency phone numbers
Police: 113
Fire: 115
Ambulance: 118

EMBASSIES AND CONSULATES
UK ☎ 02 723001
Germany ☎ 02 6231101
USA ☎ 02 290351

Netherlands ☎ 02 4855841

HEALTH ADVICE
Sun advice In northern Italy the summers can be hot and visitors should take all usual precautions against the sun – not going out in the middle of the day, wearing a hat and suncream, and drinking plenty of water.
Drugs Medicines for personal use only are allowed through customs. Many prescription and non-prescription drugs are available from pharmacies where you can get excellent advice (often in English).
Safe water Italian water is completely safe. However, because of the sterilisation processes, which can affect the taste, many people buy mineral water *(acqua minerale)*, which is readily available.

PERSONAL SAFETY

Italy has two police forces, the Polizia and the Carabinieri. The former is a standard police force, the latter a military-style force which deals with more serious crime. In practice, the visitor will be unable to distinguish between them. Visitors may also see Polizia Stradale, a specific highway force, and Vigili Urbani which operate within towns.

To help prevent crime:
● Do not carry more cash than you need
● Do not leave valuables at the poolside
● Beware of pickpockets in tourist spots or crowded places
● Avoid walking alone at night in dark alleys of the large cities
Police assistance:
☎ 113 from any call box

ELECTRICITY

The power supply in Italy is 220 volts. Power sockets are round two-holed taking plugs of two round pins. British visitors will need an adaptor and US visitors will need a voltage transformer.

OPENING HOURS

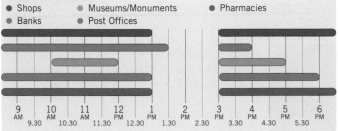

Shops (including pharmacies) sometimes open later in summer most shops close Monday morning. Post offices are usually open Saturday morning. Museums are usually open Sunday morning.

   In addition to the above, large department stores, as well as supermarkets and shops in tourist areas, may open outside these times, especially in summer.

LANGUAGE

The language you hear on the street will be Italian, even if you are on the Swiss shores of lakes Maggiore and Lugano. There are dialects in the mountains, but even there Italian is the first language. In Italian each syllable is pronounced, so *colazione* would be *col-atz-i-own-ay*. *C* and *g* are always 'hard' (as in cat or gato) before *a*, *o* or *u*, and always 'soft' (as in cello or gin) before *e* or *i*. To get a hard *c* or *g* before an *e* or *i*, Italians insert an *h*, eg Chianti. *Gn* is pronounced *ny*.

yes	*si*	good afternoon	*buongiorno*
no	*non*	goodnight	*buona sera*
please	*per favore*	how are you ?	*come sta ?*
thank you	*grazie*	do you speak	*parla inglese ?*
welcome	*benvenuto*	English?	
goodbye	*arrivederci*	I don't understand	*non capisco*
good morning	*buongiorno*	how much ?	*quanto costa ?*
bank	*banca*	cheque	*cheque*
exchange office	*cambio*	traveller's	*traveller's*
post office	*ufficio postale*	cheque	*cheque*
coin	*moneta*	credit card	*carta di credito*
banknote	*banconote*	exchange rate	*corse del cambio*
café	*caffè*	beer	*birra*
waiter	*cameriere*	wine	*vino*
waitress	*cameriera*	water	*acqua*
bill	*conto*	coffee	*caffè*
airport	*aeroporto*	boat	*battello*
train	*treno*	ticket	*biglietto*
station	*stazione*	single ticket	*andante*
bus	*autobus*	return ticket	*andante e ritorno*
bus stop	*fermata d'autobus*	car	*machina*
hotel	*albergo*	reservation	*prenotazione*
single room	*singola*	room service	*servizio nella stanza*
double room	*matrimoniale*	toilet	*gabinetto*

Best places to see

1 Bellágio

The poet Shelley claimed the 'Pearl of the Lake' was the loveliest town not only on Lake Como but in the world, and many since have agreed.

On the narrow road that runs along the eastern shore of the Como arm of Lake Como is a drive which is at best tiring, at worst positively hair-raising. By the time you get to Bellágio you may be too exhausted to notice its beauty. It is also true to say that the approach by road presents the town's poorest aspect. But the approach by water…

Bellágio sits at the very tip of the Punto Spartivento, the 'point which divides the wind', strung out along a narrow terrace on the western side. As a result, when you arrive by boat, the whole village is laid out for your inspection. The lake front is an array of beautiful buildings, red-roofed and with pastel-shaded walls, above which rises the campanile of the 11th-century church of San Giacomo.

At one end of the village is **Villa Melzi,** the finest neoclassical villa on any of the lakes. At the other end, **Villa Serbelloni,** owned by the Rockefeller Foundation, is equally impressive. Legend has it that the villa stands on the site of one of the two residences that Pliny the Younger had on the lake.

The villas may be the architectural highlights of the village, but there is much more. Though now possessing a plethora of souvenir shops – many selling locally made silk – and occasionally overcrowded because of its popularity, there is still a real Bellágio beyond the lakefront tourist traps.

A small maze of steep, sometimes cobbled streets awaits to delight and confuse. Wander at your leisure enjoying both the old-world charm and the occasional stunning views of the lake.

✚ 136 B2 ✉ The point where Lake Como splits into two 🍴 Bilacus (€€), 32 Via Serbelloni; 031 950480 🚌 Buses from Como ⛴ Regular lake boats

Villa Melzi

🕐 Gardens and chapel only Apr–Oct daily 9–6:30 ✋ Expensive

Villa Serbelloni

🕐 Gardens Apr–Oct daily. Guided tours only, at 11 and 4 ✋ Expensive

2 Duomo, Milan

Dominating the middle of Milan, and with a forest of statues, the Duomo (Cathedral) is one of the wonders of northern Italy.

On 17 September 1387 a group of Milanese armourers gathered in what is now Piazza Duomo to begin work on the building of a new cathedral for the city. The armourers were followed by the city's drapers, bootmakers, butchers and others as each

craft lent its voluntary efforts to the new building. The Duomo was built of marble from the Candoglia quarry (near Gravellona Toce, close to Lake Maggiore's western shore), the blocks of stone being marked AUF before being shipped by lake, river and canal to the city. The letters stood for *ad usum fabricae* – for building use – as the stone was exempt from local taxes, but so drawn out was the building work that *auf* became a local term for a long wait or for working for nothing. In fact, it was 400 years before the building was completed.

The Duomo Milan is 157m (171 yards) long and 92m (100 yards) wide, the third largest in the world – after St Peter's and Seville Cathedral – and has more than 3,000 statues and spires. At the highest point is the Madonnina, a gilded copper statue of the Madonna. So revered is the statue that by city regulation no building is allowed to rise above it. The Madonnina stands 108m (454ft) above the square and can be viewed at close quarters by those who climb the 919 steps, or alternatively take the lift, to the roof where the view is superb.

Inside the cathedral, a red light high in the nave marks the position of a True Nail from Christ's cross. It is brought to ground level every year so people can take a closer look. In the crypt lies the body of San Carlo Borromeo, one time archbishop of Milan whose colossal statue can be seen at Arona (➤ 71).

✚ 141 E6 ✉ Piazza Duomo, Milan ☎ 02 86463456
🕐 Mon–Fri 7–7, Sun 1:30–4:30 ♿ Free; Crypt and Treasury moderate 🍽 Al Mercante (€€), Piazza Mercanti 17; 02 8052198 🚇 1, 2

3 Isola Bella

Some are appalled by the 'wedding cake' of Isola Bella, but many more marvel at the sheer audacity of its creation. Few can stay neutral.

In 1620 the closest to the shore of the three islets off Stresa on Lake Maggiore was rocky and occupied by only a few fisherman and their families. There were two small churches, but it was a hard life for the islanders as there was almost no soil for growing food. At that time, one of the Borromean counts, who owned the islands and much of the nearby mainland, decided to transform the fishing island into a pleasure garden. He died in 1638, but his vision of creating something worthwhile from the barren rocks was taken up by his brother, Count Carlo III. Carlo had boatloads of soil transported to the island, his architect using it to create a ten-terraced island designed to look, from the shore, like a great ship sailing down the lake. The Count named the island for his wife, Isabella, but the unwieldy Isola Isabella was soon dropped in favour of today's version, which also has the advantage of translating as 'beautiful island'.

On the island the Count and his sons – the entire endeavour took decades; indeed work was not finally completed until 1958 – built a vast baroque palazzo, its numerous rooms hung with art treasures. Some of these rooms are exquisite, some exquisitely awful. The Napoleon Room (where he and Josephine slept in August 1797) and the Luca Giordano Room are peaceful and understated; the Great Hall with its Wedgwood blue walls is superb; the Tapestry Gallery with its 16th-century Flemish tapestries is extraordinary. However, the Music Room is wildly overdone and the grottoes beneath the palace, decorated with shells and curious stucco are overwhelming although the collections here are fascinating. Outside, the gardens are a treasure of overstatement. The statuary of the terraces is appalling, the whole organized in taste so bad it becomes appealing. But the gardens themselves are very good and the views are wonderful.

✚ 134 C2 ✉ Offshore from Stresa on Lake Maggiore ☎ 0323 30556 🕐 Apr–Sep daily 9–12, 1:30–5:30; Oct daily 9:30–12, 1:30–5 ✋ Expensive (combined ticket with Isola Madre available €15) 🍴 Elvezia (€€); 0323 30043 🚤 Regular lake boats from Stresa, boat 'taxis' also available

4 Listone, Verona

A short distance from the hustle and bustle of Verona's famed attractions is a quieter place where the visitor can briefly relax.

The visitors' heart of Verona is around the squares of Piazza dei Signori, with its Scaligeri tombs, and the Piazza dell'Erbe with its market stalls. From the latter it is a short step along Via Cappello to the Casa di Giulietta and Juliet's balcony.

South of the crush is Piazza Brà, the largest square in the city and one of the largest in Italy. The name is from the Latin *pratum*, meadow, and there is still an area of green at the square's heart. But it is the elegant curve of buildings along the square's western edge that holds the attention. This is the Listone, the social heart of Verona, a graceful sweep of restaurants and outdoor cafés.

At the far end of the Listone is the **Arena,** Verona's Roman amphitheatre, a vast ellipse built in the 1st century AD. From the cafés there is an excellent view of what the locals call the *ala*, meaning wing, the only section of the original three-tier perimeter wall which survived a destructive earthquake in 1183. The Arena, once the site of gladiatorial contests, is now the site of Verona's famous annual opera season. At the other end of the Listone, across Via Alpini, is the city's **Maffei Lapidary Museum,** with one of Europe's best collections of ancient inscribed stones.

✚ 139 F7 ✉ Piazza Brà, Verona 🍴 Cafe Opera (€), Piazza Brà, 10c; 045 8009903
Arena
☎ 045 8002304 🕐 Mon 1:30–7:30, Tue–Sun 8:30–7 (9–2 during the opera season) 👋 Moderate
Museo Lapidario Maffeiano
☎ 045 590087 🕐 Mon 1:30–7:30, Tue–Sun 8:30–2
👋 Moderate. Combined ticket for Arena and museum €5

5 Orta San Giúlio

Set at the bottom of a steep hill and with a marvellous view across Lake Orta, this little village is one of the prettiest on the lakes.

In the 4th century two brothers, Giúlio and Giuliani, arrived at Gozzano, near Lake Orta, to spread the gospel. Giúlio continued to the lake, drawn by the story of evil dragons that lived on an island at its heart. He amazed the locals by spreading his cloak on the water and then stepping on to it, using it as a raft. Giúlio drove the dragons away and stayed on the island, setting up a hermit's cell and preaching to the lake fishermen (➤ 84–85).

The village from which the saint set out is now known as Orta San Giúlio. It is a traffic-free, haven with steep streets and picturesque houses, some with external frescos. One such is the Casa Morgarani, the House of Dwarves, the origin of its name lost in time. The main square, Piazza Motta, is set at the lakeside. It is cool and tree-shaded, and from here you can rent boats for the short trip across to the saint's island. There are good restaurants and cafés in the square too.

The village's artistic treasure lies away from the lake, set on the hill above the houses. On the Sacre Monte a woodland path meanders past 21 chapels, which contain almost 400 life-size terracotta statues illustrating scenes in the life of St Francis of Assisi. Work on the chapels and statues began in the 17th century, but the Sacre Monte was not finally completed until early in the 19th century.

✚ 134 D2 ✉ Towards the southern end of Lake Orta's eastern shore 🖐 Free 🍴 Sacro Monte (€€), Via Sacro Monte 5; 0322 90220 🚌 There are buses along the eastern shore that link with southern Lake Maggiore and Gravellona Toce 🚢 By lake boat from Omegna

6 Piazza Vecchia, Bergamo

Although overshadowed by the reputation of Renaissance Tuscany, Bergamo is one of the finest small medieval towns in the country.

A *funivia* (a funicular or cable car) connects the modern lower city of Bergamo to the Città Alta, the Upper City, the ancient town set on a hill to the north of the new city. The ride is a short one, no more than a minute or two, but when you step out at the top you have been transported back in time by several hundred years.

Piazza Vecchia – the Old Square – is the heart of the Upper City. The architects Frank Lloyd Wright and Le Corbusier both claimed that the square was the finest in Italy dating from the Renaissance. In the middle of the piazza is the Contarini Fountain which was given to the city by Alvese Cantarini in 1780. Contarini's position as the mayor of Venice explains the fountain's embellishment with Venetian

lions. There is another Venetian lion on the Palazzo della Ragione, the magnificent building at the southern (cathedral) end of the square. The palazzo dates from the last years of the 12th century, making it the oldest municipal hall in Italy (though it needed considerable rebuilding after a fire in the 16th century). Access to the palazzo is by way of the elegant external stairway. The lion on the palazzo is a replica, the original having been torn from the building and smashed in 1796 when the townsfolk were fed up with Venetian rule.

In front of the palazzo is a statue of the poet Torquato Tasso. To the right – as you can see – is the **Torre Civica** (or Torre del Comune), the town's campanile, built in the 12th century, with a 15th-century clock. Climb the tower for a terrific view of the old town. From the Palazzo della Ragione you should cross the length of the square, marvelling at the cunning way brick has been used to create tile-effect paving, to reach the Palazzo Scamozziano which closes the northern side. This fine building was built in the 16th century in fine Palladian style.

✚ 136 D4 ✉ Bergamo's Upper Town ⑪ Colleoni e Dell'Angelo (€€€), Piazza Vecchia 7; 035 232596 🚠 Funivia from Viale Vittorio Emanuele II in the lower city

Torre Civica

☎ 035 247116 ⏰ Apr–Oct Tue–Sun 9:30–7 (9:30 Sat and hols); Nov–Mar Sat 9:30–4:30 ⑭ Inexpensive

7 Santa Caterina del Sasso

Apparently clinging to a sheer rock face above the waters of Lake Maggiore, the church of Santa Caterina is one of the most picturesque in Italy.

In the 12th century Alberto Besozzi, an unscrupulous local man who was renowned as a smuggler and money-lender, was crossing Lake Maggiore alone when a vicious storm blew up, capsizing the boat. Besozzi, flung into the water, was in danger of drowning. In terror he promised God that if his life was spared he would repent and live a blameless life of prayer. Miraculously, a wave threw him high on to a ledge on the sheer cliffs near Reno on the lake's eastern shore. Equally miraculously, he landed uninjured.

Good as his word, Besozzi spent the rest of his life – another 40 years – on the ledge, kept alive by food lowered to him in a basket by people who had heard of the miracle, and water from a spring. At one time, when plague threatened the locals, Besozzi prayed for them and they were all spared. In gratitude the locals built a church on the ledge, naming it for Santa Caterina to whom Besozzi had prayed. When he died Besozzi was buried in the church.

You can get to the church by boat but if you come by road, you will appreciate the church's unique position as you clamber down the numerous steep steps. The church at the base was damaged by a rockfall in the 17th century, but its miraculous nature was further proved when a huge boulder was stopped from demolishing the hermit's tomb by three small bricks which jammed it into a stable position. Built at the very edge of the ledge, the church is a masterpiece of grace and engineering. Inside there are beautiful medieval frescos and the remains of Besozzi – now the Blessed Alberto – curiously preserved from decay, a remarkable, if somewhat macabre, sight.

✚ 134 C3 ✉ Close to the village of Reno on Lake Maggiore's eastern shore ☎ 0332 647172 ◷ Mar–Oct daily 8:30–12, 2:30–6; Nov–Feb Sat, Sun 9–12, 2–5 🍴 Nothing at the site, but on the road to Laveno, a short distance to the north, is Il Porticciolo-Bellevue (€€); 0332 667257 🚢 Regular lake boats (otherwise a car or tour bus is essential)

35

8 Sirmione

A finger of land so narrow as to seem an unfeasible site for a town and a castle from a Hollywood film set combine to create a fairytale village.

From Lake Garda's southern shore a finger of land pokes north into the lake waters. The finger is 4km (2.5 miles) long and, at its narrowest, little more than 100m (109 yards) across. At its end is a blob of land – like the dot above an 'i'. On this area of 70ha (173 acres) sits Sirmione. The strategic importance of the isthmus was not lost on those masters of war, the Romans, but the Imperial forces had more than one reason for settling here. Just offshore, from the lake bed about 20m (66ft) below the surface, a thermal spring gushes water at 70°C (158°F); too good an opportunity for the fastidious Romans to ignore. The ruins of the Roman bath house can still be seen. They are called the **Grotte di Catullo,** named for the great lyrical poet Catullus, who is known to have had a villa here. The allusion to Catullus may be fanciful but the ruins are worth visiting: A small museum holds local Roman finds. Today the waters of the spring feed a spa that treats muscular ailments and sinus problems.

The isthmus maintained its strategic importance after the Romans departed, and in the 13th century the Scaligeri, lords of Verona, built a castle. Visitors to Sirmione must leave their cars at the apex of the 'i', and walk across a narrow bridge and through a medieval gateway which gives the impression that

the **castle** itself is being entered. In fact, it stands to the right, complete with a lake-filled moat and an intricate ring of walls which protected supply ships. The walls and towers are topped by the fish-tail battlements that were the trademark of the Scaligeri and with which visitors to Lake Garda and Verona soon become familiar.

➕ 139 E5 ✉ At the southern end of Lake Garda, close to Desenzano 🍴 Trattoria la Fiasca (€€), Via Santa Maria Maggiore 1; 030 9906111 🚌 Buses from Desenzano
🚢 Regular lake boats
Grotte di Catullo
☎ 030 916157 🕐 Mar–Oct daily 8:30–7; Nov–Feb daily 8:30–5 ✋ Moderate
Scaligeri Castle
☎ 030 916468 🕐 All year Tue–Sun 8:30–7 ✋ Moderate

⁹ Tignale/Tremósine

High above Lake Garda's western shore lie two plateaux from where there are incomparable views of the lake and a glimpse of another world.

On Lake Garda's western shore the main road (the Gardesana Occidentale) has been hewn out of the rock, sometimes tunnelling through it, sometimes set on an improbable ledge. Heading northwards with Gargagno at your back and Riva some distance ahead, you will soon reach a left turn onto a narrow, winding road which climbs to Tignale. After crossing the plateau, and the side road to Montecastello, the road descends steeply into the valley of San Michele before rising again to reach Tremósine, crossing this plateau before falling sharply to reach the main road again.

The journey is about 30km (19 miles), despite the twisting road, but it is worth the time and effort. On the Tignale road that rises from the lake there are a number of viewpoints from which to savour the panorama.

The Scaligeri, masters of
Verona, built a castle on a rock
above the village of Gárdola, but
this was destroyed and a church
raised after miracles at a nearby
chapel. Today, the sanctuary of
Madonna di Montecastello is
famed for the view and for its
art treasures.

From Tremósine, pass
through Pieve, an attractive
village with some of its
buildings perched above vast
drops. From the village the
road descends quite normally
at first, but then turns sharply
to go under itself and through
a narrow, dark chasm, offering
an extraordinary drive that
is definitely not for the
faint-hearted.

✚ 139 C6 ✉ Tignale and Tremósine
lie above Lake Garda's western shore.
They are connected to the lakeside
road, and to eath other, by narrow
roads
Madonna di Montecastello
✉ Tignale, above the western shore
of Lake Garda ☎ 0365 73019 ⊗ All
year Sun 10–12:30, 5–7 🍴 Miralago
(€), Piazza Cozzaglio 2, Tremósine;
0365 953001 🚌 Infrequent buses
from the larger lakeside towns

10 Villa Carlotta

Villa Carlotta is the most famous of the lakes' villas, and with good reason – it's a beautiful villa, elegantly decorated and with superb gardens.

Many visitors arriving at Villa Carlotta assume that the 'C' above the entrance is the C of Carlotta. It is a fair assumption, but wrong: It stands for Clerici, the family that built the villa in the 18th century. With its window-pierced façade, symmetry and entrance stairways the villa is a masterpiece. The Clerici sold the villa to the counts Sommariva, and it was during their ownership that most of the art that now graces the villa was collected. Later the villa changed hands again, being sold to a Prussian princess who gave it to her daughter Charlotte (known as Carlotta) as a wedding present. It was Carlotta who laid out the gardens in 1850s.

Inside the villa the artistic highlight is

Antonio Canova's *Cupid and Venus*, a marvellous portrayal of tenderness. The interior is also notable for its decoration, particularly the ceilings (some based on designs from Pompeii) which are masterpieces of the plasterworkers' art.

For many, though, it is the gardens that are the main attraction. Here grow more than 500 species of tree and shrub as well as fern and flower beds. There are about 150 varieties of rhododendron and azalea, many of them in Azalea Avenue or trimmed to create hedges. There are also large collections of camellias and wisterias. In summer, the flowers and shrubs make Carlotta the most vivid place on the lakes, while the citrus trees add a sharp tang to the air.

🚹 136 B2 ✉ Tremezzo, on the western shore of Lake Como
☎ 0344 40405 🕐 Apr–Sep daily 9–6; Mar–Oct daily
9:30–11:00, 2–4:30 🎟 Expensive 🍴 Tremezzino (€€), Via
Regina 40, Bolvedro; 0344 40496 🚌 Buses along the shore
road from Como ⛴ Regular boat service

Exploring

With the Alps to the west and north, the Dolomites to the east, and the plain of the River Po to the south, the Italian Lakes occupy an enviable position. Abundant water from the mountains, and equally abundant sunshine have created ideal growing conditions allowing the establishment of world-famous gardens. The equable winter climate attracted the rich and famous, whose villas added to the architectural and artistic richness of an area already wealthy because it lay on the trade route from Venice to northern Europe. With fine cities and towns, an array of delightful villages, fine Italian cooking, and endless opportunities for water and other sports, the Italian Lakes are among the most interesting and exciting destinations in Europe. And to cap it all, just a short distance south is Milan, economic powerhouse of Italy and fashion capital of the world.

Milan

Milan, Italy's second city but its unquestioned economic hub, deserves a book of its own. There is a Roman city, *Mediolanum*, named after its position at the heart of the Lombardy Plain and one whose early Christian monuments rival those of any other town. There is the Milan of the Viscontis and Sforzas, that of the Spanish domination and another from the Austrian era. There are marvellous palazzos from the 18th and 19th centuries and the modern commercial city. There is even the Milan whose soccer teams are the equal of any in Europe and whose stadium at San Siro is worth visiting just to be amazed at its size and elegance.

Which of these cities should be explored by the visitor on a time budget? Perhaps a little of each – the 'must-see' sights which, hopefully, are covered here. As with all large, commercially active cities, Milan can be all pace and movement. But at its heart, in Piazza Duomo and the nearby squares, the Italians find, as always, time for a coffee and a moment's relaxation away from the hustle.

✚ 136 F1

BASILICA DI SANT'AMBROGIO

Legend has it that Ambrogio (St Ambrose) arrived in Milan soon after the city's bishop had died. The contest for a successor was causing feuding and uproar. Ambrogio calmed the crowd, and they were so impressed with his bearing that they decided he should be the new bishop. Ambrogio was not even a Christian at the time, but was hastily baptized and installed as bishop. Soon after, he began work on the church which now bears his name. The present church, a lovely building in Romanesque style, dates from the 11th century although there are sections of much earlier work. Inside, the gold altar by Volvinio, with its relief panels depicting scenes in the life of the saint, is a masterpiece of 9th-century goldsmithing.

🔁 *140 E2* ✉ Piazza Sant'Ambrogio ☎ 02 86450895 🕐 Tue–Sun 9:30–12, 2:30–6 🖐 Free 🚇 M2, S Ambrogio

BIBLIOTECA (PINACOTECA) AMBROSIANA

The vast Palazzo dell'Ambrosiana was begun in the early 17th century to house the library of Cardinal Federico Borromeo, a member of the family which owned, among other things, the islands in Lake Maggiore. The building is a little severe, but inside there is an excellent collection of art as well as the library. The collection includes works by Brueghel, Caravaggio and Luini, but is most notable for the portrait of the musician Gaffurio by Leonardo da Vinci.

🔁 *141 E5* ✉ Piazza Pio XI. Near to Piazza Duomo ☎ 02 806921 🕐 Tue–Sun 10–5:30 🖐 Expensive

CASTELLO SFORESCO

The first castle on this site was built by the Viscontis from the mid-14th century. This building was partially destroyed by the townsfolk on the downfall of the family, but their joy must have been short-lived as the Sforzas soon rose to power and created an even more domineering structure. The Sforza fortress fell into disrepair but was saved from demolition by enlightened citizens and now houses superb collections of art, weapons and armour, and much more. Of the art, pride of place must go to the awesome *Rondanini Pietà* by Michelangelo, while the collection of weapons is one of the finest in Europe. The castle is also worth visiting just for the building itself. Look up as you enter the Torre dell'Orologio, the Clock Tower. This superb 70m (230ft) tower is an exact replica of the 15th-century original, destroyed when the gunpowder stored within exploded.

✚ *140 C3* ✉ Piazza Castello ☎ 02 88463700 🕐 Tue–Sun 9–5:30 🚇 M1, Cairoli station ♿ Free

DUOMO
Best places to see, ➤ 24–25.

MUSEO NAZIONALE DELLA SCIENZA E DELLA TECNOLOGIA LEONARDO DA VINCI

The museum named after Leonardo houses not only an excellent collection exploring science and engineering but a gallery dealing with his work in aeronautics, engineering and anatomy. The 'conventional' section of the museum includes full-size ships, planes and trains, and exhibits such as the equipment used by Umberto Nobile on his balloon-borne expedition to the North Pole.

www.museoscienza.org

➕ *140 E1* ✉ Via San Vittore 21 ☎ 02 48010040 🕐 Tue–Sat 9:30–4:50 (6:30 on Sat and Sun) 💶 Expensive Ⓜ M2, S Ambrogio

PINACOTECA DI BRERA

Palazzo di Brera was begun in the early 16th century and is in fine baroque style with a unity that belies the fact that it took more than 100 years to complete. In the courtyard is a bronze statue of Napoleon by Canova. This fine work is a prelude to the collection inside which many consider to be one of the best in Italy. Everyone will have a favourite, but by common consent the finest works are the heartbreaking *Dead Christ* by Andreas Mantegna; and the *Madonna with Saints*, which includes the famous portrait of Federico di Montelfeltro (and his equally famous nose) by Piero della Francesca.

🕂 *141 B5* ✉ 28 Via Brera ☎ 02 89421146 🕐 Tue–Sun 8:30–7 💷 Moderate 🚇 M2, Lanza

SANTA MARIA DELLE GRAZIE

In 1463 the Dominican Order of friars was given land on which to build a church and monastery. The church, dedicated to St Mary of the Favours, is built in dramatic style with a marvellous façade and apse. It has two surviving cloisters, the Cloister of the Dead and the smaller Cloister of the Frogs. The church is well worth visiting, but its famed treasure is within the nondescript building beside it, once the refectory of the monastery. Here in 1495 Leonardo da

Vinci began work on his *Last Supper*, which, together with the *Mona Lisa*, have set the seal on his reputation as an artist. Always the innovator, Leonardo chose to paint on to dry plaster rather than using the more common technique of painting quickly on to wet plaster. Though this allowed him more time – it took two years to complete the work – it meant that moisture between the plaster and the paint lifted flakes of paint off the wall. Within 20 years the painting had begun to deteriorate. There have been several attempts at restoration and the last has only just been completed.

🕆 *140 D1* ✉ Cenacolo Vinciano (Leonardo's Last Supper), Piazza Santa Maria delle Grazie ☎ 02 4987588 🕐 Tue–Sat 9–7; Sun 9–8 💷 Expensive 🚇 M1, Conciliazione ❓ Booking a time to see the fresco is now obligatory (02 89421146 for reservations)

VILLA REALE
(VILLA BELGIOJOSO BONAPARTE)

Built in neoclassical style and once owned by Napoleon, the Villa Reale, standing at the edge of Milan's Public Gardens, is now the city's museum of modern art. The rooms are a marvel of 18th-century elegance, with chandeliers, parquet floors and sumptuous plasterwork, to such an extent that the works, illustrating the artistic movements of the late 19th and early 20th centuries, can seem a little out of place. Many are by north Italian artists, but there are also paintings by Cézanne, Renoir, Gauguin, Picasso and Matisse. After exploring the museum, go to the back of the villa. The rear façade is by far the best and can be viewed across a delightful lake.

🕆 *141 B8* ✉ Via Palestro 16 ☎ 02 76002819 🕐 Daily 9–5:30 💷 Free 🚇 M1, Palestro

a walk around Milan's highlights

Start in front of the Duomo (➤ 24–25) in Piazza Duomo.

Facing the Duomo, bear right to walk along the side of the building. This is Via Arcivescovado, though you will not see this displayed. To the right is Palazzo Reale.

Palazzo Reale must not be confused with Villa Reale (➤ 51). It was once the Ducal Palace of the Viscontis and was partially destroyed by fire but renovated and added to over the years. Mozart's first opera was performed here when he was 14 years old. The *palazzo* houses the Museo del Duomo, a collection of religious objects.

Continue along the road, on the right is San Gottardo with its beautiful campanile. Turn left behind the cathedral. To the right is the Palazzo Arcivescovile, built in 1170, while ahead is Piazza Fontana. At the end of the cathedral, turn left to return to the main square. Turn right through the Galleria Vittorio Emanuele.

The Milanese refer to the Galleria as *Il salotto di Milano*, the drawing room of Milan, because its cafés and restaurants are meeting places. The exclusive Savini's is where crowds assemble after the first night at La Scala.

Exit the Galleria into Piazza della Scala. The opera house is to the left. Ahead is a statue of Leonardo da Vinci.

a walk

Walk on, with Palazzo Marino to the right, then turn right to reach one side of the church of San Fedele. Step right into Piazza San Fedele.

San Fedele is the most complete of Milan's 16th-century churches. It was built by San Carlo Borromeo (➤ 71) and outside is a monument to Alessandro Manzoni (➤ 101).

Go back to the side of the church and bear left across the road to reach the Casa degli Omenoni.

Casa degli Omenoni is the House of Giants, named after the eight caryatids sculpted on the outside by Leone Leoni for whom the house was built in 1565.

Continue past the House of Giants (along Via degli Omenoni), to Piazza Belgioioso, turning left along it.

Palazzo Belgioioso was built for a family whose name is carved in the piazza outside. Farther on, to the left, is a museum in Manzoni's home from 1814 until his death.

Continue along Via Gerollamo Morone from the end of the square to reach Via Alessandro Manzoni. Turn right towards the Poldi-Pezzoli Museum.

In a fine 17th-century palazzo, this is one of Italy's foremost museums. Art includes *Profile of a Young Woman* by Pollaiolo and works by Luini, Mantegna and Botticelli.

Turn left along Via Alessandro Manzoni, soon reaching Piazza della Scala again.

La Scala opera house was built in 1778, taking its name from the Scaligeri family. In its early days the theatre was mostly used as a gaming house but its reputation was transformed with the rise of Verdi. Today La Scala is one of the world's great opera houses. There is a museum about the theatre.

Pass the theatre, crossing Via Santa Margherita, Via San Protaso and the tram lines of Via Tommaso Grossi. Go under the arch and across the pedestrianized road to Piazza dei Mercanti.

On the street side is the Palazzo della Ragione, its arcaded lower floor once a market, its upper storeys the town hall and law courts. Opposite is the Palazzo delle Scuole Palatine, a 17th-century school of mathematics, rhetoric and law, beside the 14th-century marble Loggia degli Osii.

Now take the few steps back to Piazza Duomo.

Distance 2km (1.25 miles)
Time 1–3 hours, depending on museums visited
Start/End Point In front of the Duomo in Piazza Duomo
✚ *141 E6*
Lunch Al Mercante (€€) ✉ Piazza Mercanti 17 ☎ 02 8052198
Museo del Duomo
✉ Piazzo Duomo ◷ Daily 9:30–12:30, 3–6 ☎ 02 860358
✋ Inexpensive
Casa del Manzoni
✉ Via Morone 1 ☎ 02 86460403 ◷ Tue–Fri, Sun 9–12, 2–4 ✋ Free
Museo Poldi-Pezzoli
✉ Via Manzoni 12 ☎ 02 794889 ◷ Tue–Sun 10–6. Early closing Sun afternoons (summer) ✋ Expensive
Museo Teatrale alla Scala
✉ Piazza della Scala ☎ 02 8053418 ◷ 9–12, 2–5 (closed Sun Nov–Apr) ✋ Moderate

Western Lakes

Close to Mont Blanc there is a mountain peak (Mont Dolent) where France, Switzerland and Italy touch. From it the high ridge of the Alps heads north-westwards and eastwards and the country borders follow it. The Matterhorn lies on the border between Switzerland and Italy, as does Monte Rosa. From Monte Rosa the high ridge and the border turn northeast towards the Simplon Pass. On the Italian side of the ridge the land falls away swiftly – it is barely 60km (37 miles) from the second highest summit in the Alps to the edge of the Lombardy Plain.

This is the Italian region of Piemonte (Piedmont), a name which translates, accurately, as the foot of the mountains. The whole of Lake Orta and the western shore of Lake Maggiore lie within the region, the eastern shore lying in Lombardy. Border crossings are usually very relaxed, but remembering the passport is critical just in case the Swiss let you in but the Italians are reluctant to return the favour later in the day. It is also worth taking insurance documents for your car as occasionally the border police will ask for them and have been known to refuse entry to drivers who don't have them.

Lake Lugano

Lugano is shaped like a fox, its long bushy tail and its head shared by Switzerland and Italy, its legs firmly anchored on Swiss soil. The city of Lugano and the northern shore of the lake were once part of the city state of Milan, but the Swiss took both the city and adjacent land in 1512. When Italy was freed from Austrian rule and unified, no claim was made on Milan's former territories and, despite the common language and the oddity of Campione, no serious attempt has ever been made to regain the northern shore. As a result, Italian Lake Lugano is fragmented: there is a small section of the southwestern shore, the enclave of Campione and a larger section of the eastern lake.

✚ 135 C5

CAMPIONE D'ITALIA

In the 8th century the local lord of this part of Lake Lugano gave in perpetuity the land which is now Campione to the church of Sant'Ambrogio in Milan. Remarkably, when the Swiss annexed Milanese holdings on the northern shores of the lake they respected the original covenant and made no attempt to take the village which had grown up on the church's holding. During the struggles of Austrian rule over parts of north Italy and the wars of the Risorgimento, Switzerland made no attempt to absorb the village. And so, despite the fact that the village – which now has grown into a town – is entirely surrounded by Switzerland, it remains resolutely Italian. Of necessity, Campione uses the Swiss postal system and all the shops and restaurants accept Swiss money, but this is very much an Italian town. A plan to link the town with Italy by building a cable car from it to Sighignola, a small village near Lanzo d'Intelvi, failed so Campione's unique position, reachable only from Switzerland, will continue for many years. The town now makes the most of its position by having a **casino.**

Visitors to Campione are left in little doubt about the unusual nature of the town when they are greeted by a huge arch and elaborate fountain. In medieval times the town was famous for the Maestri Campionesi, a group of architects, builders and sculptors who were renowned for the quality of their work. The group built Sant'Ambrogio in Milan, Modena Cathedral and the more modest, but no less beautiful, church here.

➕ 135 C5 ✉ An Italian enclave on Lake Lugano's eastern shore
🚌 Infrequent buses from Switzerland 🚢 Regular lake steamers
🍴 Da Candida (€€), Via Marco 4; 091 6497541

Casino

✉ Campione d'Italia ☎ 091 6401111 🕐 All year daily, restaurant open at 12, gaming tables at 3pm

PONTE TRESA

Unsurprisingly Ponte Tresa is the bridge that crosses the Tresa river, the outflow of Lake Lugano flowing west to Lake Maggiore. The bridge, a five-arched, red granite structure, is also the border between Italy and Switzerland, and so there are actually two towns, both called Ponte Tresa. Italian Ponte Tresa is usually a traffic bottleneck – ignore the chaos and park early to enjoy the lakefront on the eastern side of the village, a delightful area. Take a stroll around the rest of the village and peruse its shops.

✚ 134 C4 ✉ At the western end of Lake Lugano's southern shore

PORTO CERESIO

Following two sides of a square-cut bay of Lake Lugano, Porto Ceresio is a lovely place. The village is renowned for the views along the two arms of Lugano and across the lake to Morcote, but don't ignore Porto Ceresio itself. There is nothing of great note here – a huddle of pretty houses and the little harbour of the same name – but it encapsulates the elegance of older, less 'touristy' lakes. From the village a road heads south towards Varese, soon reaching Besano, famous for the local rocks – one of Italy's most important sources of Triassic fossils – there is a **fossil museum.** The same road leads to Bisuchio, where the 16th-century Villa Cicogna Mozzoni is a national monument. The villa has an arcaded ground floor, frescoes and stands in Italian-style gardens.

✛ 135 C5 ✉ Close to the Swiss border on the southern shore of Lake Lugano

Museo Paleontologico

✉ Via Prestini, Besano ✉ 0332 919200 ⏰ Apr–Sep Mon–Fri 10–12, Sat–Sun 11–12:30, 2:30–6:30; Oct–Mar Mon–Fri 9:30–12:30, Sun 2:30–6:30 ✋ Inexpensive 🚌 Buses from Varese

VARESE AND SURROUNDINGS

The large, modern city of Varese is built on flat land below Monte Campo dei Fiori. It is a prosperous place, famous for its shoemaking, but has other light industries and a reputation as a 'garden city' because of its parks and the lushness of the local valleys.

Within the city, which is worth visiting for its wealth of modern shops, be sure to see Del Bernascove, the campanile, 72m (236ft) high, which stands at the heart of the old town and is a symbol of Varese. There is an interesting complex of religious buildings beside the campanile. One, the 12th-century baptistery of San Giovanni, is a national monument. Nearby, the baroque Palazzo Estense is another national monument. It was built in the mid-18th century by Francesco II Este, Duke of Modena, and is situated in an extensive natural park but fronted by formal gardens.

From Varese, Monte Campo dei Fiori can be visited for a view of the picturesque village of Santa Maria del Monte, or the local lakes and valleys can be explored. Lake Varese is the largest of the three lakes between the city and Lake Maggiore. On the lake's island, Isolina Virginia, excavations have revealed prehistoric remains of enormous importance. Of the valleys, the Valganna, which takes the main road to Ponte Tresa, is the most scenic, with small lakes and

fine woodland, but the Valcuvia –
between Varese and Lake Maggiore – is
the most interesting. From it a side road
climbs steeply to **Arcumeggia,** where,
from the 1950s, contemporary artists
have frescoed the outside walls of the
houses to create an open-air art gallery.
The works are not of the highest quality
perhaps, but the idea is great fun.

South of Varese, Castiglione Olona
should be visited to see one of
Lombardy's most important **complexes
of medieval buildings.** In the early
15th century Cardinal Branda
Castiglioni, a local man, built a palazzo
for himself, a house for his parents,
a domed church, a baptistery and a
collegiate church. He commissioned
the master artist Masoline de Panicale
to paint frescoes on the churches and
baptistery.There is a small museum
devoted to the history of the site.

✚ 134 D4

Arcumeggia

✉ At top of steep road from the Valcuvia; car
or taxi essential, but parking can be difficult

☎ 0332 283604

Church Complex/Museum

✉ Castiglione Olona. On the N233 (Milano)
road south of Varese ☎ 0331 858301

🕐 Tue–Sun 9–12, 3–6 ✋ Moderate

🍽 Colombo Rosella (€€), Via Cesare Battisti
112, Castiglione Olona; 0331 859275

🚌 Infrequent buses

Swiss Lake Lugano

A large portion of Lake Lugano lies in the Swiss canton of Ticino. Here you can easily spend a day or two exploring the elegant, modern city of Lugano, and the lovely scenery and towns nearby.

LUGANO

Most of Lugano's highlights lie close to the lake. At the southern end of the city is Paradiso, a suburb of new hotels, good restaurants, nightclubs and shops. Heading north, you are soon in the old quarter of the city with its narrow streets and large open squares. Here, the church of Santa Maria Degli Angioli has frescoes by Bernardino Luini, pupil of Leonardo and, some maintain, the equal of his master. The paintings are some of Luini's best. From Piazza Luini, in which the church stands, follow Via Nassa north. The surrealist sculpture in Piazzetta San Carlo is *The Dignity of Time* by Salvador Dalí. Via Nassa leads to Piazza della Riforma, with its cafés and the impressive town hall. The square is one of the main venues for Lugano's famous Jazz Festival each June. Cross to the lakeside and continue towards Parco Civico. Inland from here is Quartière Maghetti, a modern district of shops and restaurants. On the edge of the Quartière is the **Museo Cantonale d'Arte,** which displays contemporary art and holds regular exhibitions showing the work of all Swiss, but chiefly Ticino, artists. Until recently Villa Favorita housed the Thyssen-Bornemisza collection of paintings, one of the best private collections in the world. The bulk of the collection is now in Madrid. Some works do remain, but at present the villa is closed, although the magnificent gardens are occasionally open to the public.

✠ 135 C5

Museo Cantonale d'Arte
✉ Lugano ☎ 091 9104780 ◉ Wed–Sun 10–5, Tue 2–5 ♿ Expensive

MELIDE AND SOUTH OF LUGANO

Heading south from Lugano there are several interesting places on the northern shores of the lake. At Melide, **Swissminiatur** is a replica of all the main sites in Switzerland set out on an area of 1ha (2.5 acres). From Melide a *funivia* takes visitors to Carona where there is a fine park and a church with 16th-century frescoes. Further on, Morcote is often called the 'Pearl of the Lake'. With its narrow streets of arcaded houses and the beautiful setting of the church of Santa Maria del Sasso among tall cypresses, it is easy to see why. Elsewhere on the peninsula of land which ends at Morcote, admirers of the books of Herman Hesse can make a pilgrimage to Gentilino where he is buried. Farther from Lugano, and across the lake, at Capolago, a **rack railway** takes visitors to the top of Monte Generoso, a much higher peak, with expansive views. From the top, walkers can explore an alpine landscape rich in wildflowers.

✚ 135 C5

Swissminiatur

✉ Melide ☎ 091 6401060 🕐 Daily mid-Mar to Oct 9–6 💷 Expensive
🍽 There is a café at the site

Rack Railway to Monte Generoso

✉ Capolago ☎ 091 6481105 🕐 Daily May–Oct 10–6 💷 Expensive
🍽 Café at the top (€)

MONTE BRÉ AND EAST OF LUGANO

From Lugano a funicular climbs Monte Bré, to the north. The sunny peak is renowned for its view and as a starting point for walks. Another funicular, from Paradiso, goes to Monte San Salvatore, where the view includes not only the lake and the city, but the Valais Alps and the Bernese Oberland. To the east of Lugano, at Gandria, a fascinating **museum** explores the work of the Swiss customs and the ingenious methods used by smugglers to bring contraband in and out of Switzerland. The most bizarre item is a submarine whose torpedo tubes were filled with salami.

✉ 135 C5
Museo Doganale Svizzero (Smuggling Museum)
✉ Gandria ☎ 091 9239843 ⏱ Aug daily 1:30–5:30 ✋ Moderate
🍴 Limited locally, but there is a good choice in Lugano

Lake Maggiore

As with Lake Lugano, you will find that to do a full circuit of the lake – a distance of 170km (105 miles), rather too far to travel if justice is to be done to the places along the way – you will need to take your passports with you, as such a trip will cross into and out of Switzerland.

✚ 134 C3

ANGERA

This small town tucked into a cove of Lake Maggiore's south-eastern shore has a lovely lakefront walk shaded by chestnut trees. The local **museum** explores the town's interesting history, noting that Pietro Martire, the chronicler of Columbus's journey to the New World, was a local man. Though the town is pleasant, most visitors come to see the forbidding *rocca* (castle) that looms above it – visit the town by boat for a real appreciation of just how impressive and well situated this formidable fortress really is. It was built by the Borromean family in the 15th century and was cleverly designed to ensure that attacks invariably turned the attackers' unprotected right side towards the defenders. Inside it is unfurnished, its gaunt appearance adding to its sinister qualities, though some rooms have surprisingly subtle frescoes. The **castle** is now the home of an excellent **doll museum** which concentrates on European dolls from the 19th century to the present day.

✚ 134 D3 ✉ At the southern end of Lake Maggiore's eastern shore 🍴 Bacco (€€), Via Mazzini, 71; 0331 930232

Town Museum

✉ Via Marconi, Angera ☎ 0332 931133/391915 🕓 Mon, Thu, Sat 3–7 ✋ Free 🚌 Regular buses along the eastern shore ⛴ Regular lake boats

Castle and Doll Museum

✉ At top of steep hill from town, car or taxi essential ☎ 0332 931300 🕓 Mar–Sep daily 9:30–6; Oct–Nov daily 9:30–5 ✋ Inexpensive 🍴 None on site, but lots of choice in the town

ARONA

Standing across the lake from Angera, Arona owes its prosperity to the age of railways, as it stands at the point where the line from Switzerland through the Simplon Tunnel meets the line linking Milan to Turin. This economically strategic position is reflected in the array of fine 19th-century houses. One older building, the Palazzo de Filippi, houses a **museum** which explores the town's history. There was a **castle** here too, its defenders staring across the lake at those in Angera's stronghold, but little now remains.

Just outside Arona stands the colossal **statue of San Carlo Borromeo.** The saint was born in Arona Castle in 1538, was appointed Cardinal at 22 and was Archbishop of Milan by the time he was 26. Though the fact that his uncle was Pope Pius IV may have helped his promotion, he was undoubtedly a devout and hard-working man. After his death a member of his family decided that Carlo deserved a memorial befitting his stature. The original idea envisaged 15 chapels surrounding a vast statue, though only three were begun and only one completed. The statue is 23.5m (77ft) tall, stands on a plinth 12m (40ft) high, and is apparently a good likeness of the man, right down to his huge nose. Visitors can climb up within for a precarious view from inside the head, but since the statue is made of bronze it can be very hot in summer.

✚ 134 D2 ✉ At the southern end of Lake Maggiore's western shore

Town Museum

✉ Palazzo de Filippi, Arona ☎ 0322 242577 🕐 By request only 🖐 Free
🍴 Pescatori (€€), Via Marconi 27; 032 248312 🚌 Infrequent buses along the western shore 🚢 Regular lake boats

Rocca di Arona (castle remains)

✉ Above the town to the west ☎ 0322 243601 🕐 Apr, May daily 2–5; Jun–Oct daily 10–7:30 🖐 Free 🚌 No buses, so car or taxi required

Statue of San Carlo Borromeo

✉ North of Arona ☎ 0322 242488 🕐 Mar–Sep daily 9:30–6; Oct, Nov daily 9:30–5 🖐 Inexpensive 🚌 Regular buses along the western shore
🚢 Regular lake boats

BORROMEAN ISLANDS

Offshore from Stresa (▶ 80–81) on Lake Maggiore's western shore lie three small islands. The most famous of these is Isola Bella, but the other two are also worth visiting.

Isola Bella

Best places to see, ▶ 26–27.

Isola Madre

The largest island, and the one furthest from Stresa, is Isola Madre, the Mother Island. Here the Borromeo family built a single villa, landscaping the parkland around it. The villa is decorated in a much more subdued and relaxed style than its neighbour on Isola Bella. The chapel beside it houses the tombs of many members of the Borromeo family, reflecting the fact that Madre was a place where the family lived rather than where they impressed their rivals. The island's parkland is a treasure house of rare species including a Kashmir cypress, said to be the finest specimen in Europe. There are also rows of citrus plants scenting the air, and a tropical greenhouse.

✚ 134 C2 ✉ Offshore from Stresa and Pallanza ☎ 0323 31261
🌐 Easter–Oct daily 9–12, 1:30–5:30 ✋ Expensive 🍴 La Piratera (€€), Isola
Madre; 032 331171 🛥 Regular lake boats from both Stresa and Pallanza
❓ Visitors cannot land on the island unless they purchase an entry ticket

Isola dei Pescatori

This, as the name implies, is the fisherman's island, the only one
of the Borromean trio which reflects the original occupation of the
islands. While the Borromeo family was transforming Isola Bella
and laying claim to Isola Madre for their private villa, Pescatori was
owned by the Archbishop of Novara, who refused to give it up. It
is a marvellous place with fishing boats – the traditional *lucia* with
which all visitors to the lakes soon become familiar – at the
harbour edge, and nets hung over the walls to dry in the sun.
The island is entirely occupied by a village which is achingly
picturesque and, apart from the area where boats drop visitors,
is free of souvenir shops. At the heart of the village stands the
11th-century church with its neat conical spire.

✚ 134 C2 ✉ Offshore from Stresa 🍴 La Peschiera (€€), Via Lungo Lago 6;
0323 933808 🛥 Regular boats from Stresa

CÁNNERO RIVIERA

Cánnero was once described as the 'Genoese Riviera in miniature', a fact which prompted the town fathers to add Riviera to the name and to style itself as the 'Nice of Maggiore' because of the mildness of its winter climate. It was also described as 'a pearl in a bracket of villas and vineyards', a description that is much less appropriate today as the vineyards have all but gone. The villas remain, though. Garibaldi stayed in one, Villa Sabbioncella, after the battle of Luino during his Risorgimento campaign. Neither that villa nor any other is open to visitors, who must content themselves with an exploration of the huddle of narrow streets, each lined with fine houses. All explorations are likely to end at the little harbour from which there is a view of the two small Cánnero or Malpaga islands, each of which is topped by the ruins of a castle.

The castles date from the 12th century and were once occupied by a band of five brothers who terrorized the local villages and pirated any ship unfortunate enough to come too close. Eventually the Viscontis became fed up with this blatant display of lawlessness, though it took them six months to force the brothers out of their strongholds before destroying the castles.

➕ 134 B4 ✉ On the western shore of Lake Maggiore to the north of Verbania 🍴 Il Cartile (€€), Via Massimo d'Azeglio 73; 0323 787213
🚌 Regular bus service along the western shore ⛴ Regular lake steamers

CANNÓBIO

Though sadly split in two by the main road up Maggiore's western shore, Cannóbio is still worth a visit. On the lakeside, narrow, picturesque streets lead to the Santuario della Pietà which houses a painting that allegedly started bleeding in 1522. The chapel is the work of Pellegrini, a famous 16th-century architect who was commissioned by San Carlo Borromeo himself. The two men's involvement is an indication of the effect the miracle had on the area. On the mountain side of the main road, a minor road reaches the *orrido* of Sant'Anna. An *orrido* is a tight gorge through which a noisy stream rushes, in this case the Torrente Cannóbio, which reaches the lake at the town. Close to the gorge is the neat church after which it is named.

➕ 134 B4 ✉ The first town in Italy if travelling south from Switzerland along Lake Maggiore's western shore 🍴 Sant'Anna (€€), at the *orrido;* 0323 70682
🚌 Infrequent bus service along the western shore ⛴ Regular lake steamers

LAVENO

Visitors who use the car ferry to cross Lake Maggiore from Verbania to Laveno are treated to a magnificent view of the town, which is dominated by the church of Santi Giacomo e Felipe, built only in the 1930s and on a very grand scale with a huge dome. Those arriving by boat will also note the curious yellow buckets that travel slowly up the hillside behind the town. The fact that Laveno has an industrial suburb – Mombello – might imply that these are part of a quarrying operation. In fact they are the transporters of one the lakes' area's most exciting *funivias* (a type of cable car). Each car carries two people, and though the gate in is securely fixed there is no other protection. Although you may need nerves of steel to take this ride it does allow a good view of the brightly hued butterflies that congregate along the swathe of scrub cut through the forest below the *funivia*. The view from Sasso del Ferro at the top is magnificent.

🏛 134 C3 ✉ On Lake Maggiore's eastern shore
🚌 Infrequent buses along lake's eastern shore 🚢 Regular lake steamers. Car ferry (and foot passengers) from Verbania

Funivia

☎ 0332 668012 🕐 Apr–Sep daily 9:30–6 (Sat, Sun and holidays until 7); Oct–Mar Sat, Sun and holidays 9:30–5 ✋ Moderate

LUINO

This delightful small town has two claims to fame. It was the first place in Italy to raise a statue in honour of Giuseppe Garibaldi, the hero of the Risorgimento. Garibaldi came to the town to raise another army after he had been defeated by the Austrians at the battle of Custozza. This event, and other aspects of the town's history, are explored in a **museum** in Palazzo Verbania. The statue stands in Piazza Garibaldi (of course) where, on Wednesdays, a

market is held. The second claim is that the great artist Bernardino Luini was born here. A painting of the *Adoration of the Magi* in the church of San Pietro – at the eastern, uphill section of the town – is attributed by some experts to the artist. In the church of Madonna del Carmine beside the main lakeside road there are frescos that are the work of pupils of Luini.

✠ 134 C4 ✉ On Lake Maggiore's eastern shore 🚌 Infrequent buses along lake's eastern shore 🚢 Regular lake steamers 🍴 Il Porticciolo-Bellevue (€€€), Via Fortino 40 (about 1.5km/1 mile north); 0332 667257

Town Museum
✉ Palazzo Verbania ☎ 0332 532057/543564 🕐 Mon 2–6:30, Sat 8:30–12
✋ Free

PALLANZA

Pallanza is just one of three villages – the others are Intra and Verbania – which make up a complex usually known as Verbania. The other two villages form a semi-industrialized town and ferry port (Lake Maggiore's only car ferry links Verbania to Laveno), but Pallanza is sufficiently removed to maintain a degree of individuality.

The old village has the usual maze of narrow streets lined with fine houses. It has a long-standing reputation as an autumn and winter resort, and as a place where the flowers and shrubs seem to bloom even more vividly than elsewhere. The latter led to the village being referred to as the 'cradle of flowers' in old guides to the lake. Pallanza as a resort is mentioned in the classic Hemingway book *A Farewell to Arms*, where the characters planned 'to go to Pallanza. It is beautiful there when, in autumn, the leaves change their colour…There is a nice village at Pallanza and you can row out to the islands where the fishermen live…'

Palazzo Dugnani, a fine 18th-century building in the old quarter, is now the Museo del Paesaggio, the museum of landscapes, with a collection of paintings and frescoes. The real treasure here, however, lies just outside the village.

Villa Taranto, a garden of 16ha (40 acres) beside the road that links Pallanza with Verbania, is one of the world's great

gardens. The villa is named after the Duke of Taranto, one of Napoleon's generals. He was an ancestor of Scotsman Neil McEachern, who renamed it when he bought the property early in the 20th century. McEachern created a garden of awesome splendour. It is criss-crossed by 8km (5 miles) of paths and has more than 20,000 varieties of trees and shrubs from all over the world. Some of these specimens are the only examples in Europe. There are also ponds and a greenhouse with rainforest plants. In spring the garden's Tulip Week, when over 80,000 tulips are in bloom, draws crowds from all over the world. A little later in the season, the blooming of the azaleas and rhododendrons is another highlight.

🚹 134 C3 ✉ Part of the Verbania complex of towns/ villages on Lake Maggiore's western shore 🍴 Il Torchio (€€), Via Manzoni 20; 0323 503352 🚌 Infrequent buses along lake's western shore 🛳 Regular lake steamers

Villa Taranto
☎ 0323 404555 🕑 Gardens only Mar–Oct daily 8:30–6 or sunset
✋ Moderate

SANTA CATERINA DEL SASSO
Best places to see, ➤ 34–35.

STRESA
Stresa is the most elegant of all Lake Maggiore's towns, and its lakeside gardens are evidence of a prosperity mirrored in the array of substantial hotels. Of these hotels, the finest is the very grandly (if curiously) named Grand Hotel et des Iles Borromées, one of just two on the lakes which lie outside the Italian hotel classification system because they are too luxurious merely to be five-star (the other is the Villa d'Este at Cernobbio on Lake Como). It was in this hotel that Hemingway had Frederick Henry stay to escape the war in *A Farewell to Arms*. It is interesting that for being so elegant and

well-known a town – Stresa has a famous annual music festival and is frequently home to conferences and conventions – it is such a tiny place and has so few attractions within its boundaries. There are some good shops and the usual range of souvenir outlets; and Piazza Cadorna, the central square, with its outdoor cafés is excellent, but that is all. The town is a fine base for local excursions, though.

To the north is the lower station of the *funivia* to the Mottarone, from which there is a view of Monte Rosa. On clear days Milan's Duomo and the Matterhorn are visible. The *funivia* makes a stop at the **alpine garden** near Gignese, where thousands of species of alpine flower have been planted since 1934. From the garden there is a splendid view of the lake. Beyond the *funivia,* Baveno is a very pleasant village with a 12th-century Romanesque façade and campanile. Beside the church is a baptistery with 15th-century frescoes. Baveno became a socialite resort after Queen Victoria stayed for a week in 1879. South of Stresa is **Villa Pallavicino.** The 19th-century villa is not open to the public, but its 12ha (30 acres) of parkland is. Here, there are formal gardens, but the most entertaining feature is the safari-style zoo, where the animals enjoy minimal caging and there is good access for children to the docile species.

🕂 134 C2 ✉ On Lake Maggiore's western shore 🍴 Piemontese (€€), Via Mazzini 25; 0323 30235 🚌 Infrequent buses along lake's western shore 🚢 Regular lake steamers

Giardino Alpino

✉ Gignese ☎ 0323 31308 🕔 Apr to mid-Oct Tue–Sun 9–6 👎 Inexpensive

Villa Pallavicino

☎ 0323 31533 🕔 Mar–Oct daily 9–6 👎 Expensive

Swiss Lake Maggiore

The northern end of Lake Maggiore lies in Switzerland. Visitors who head north along the western shore will cross the border soon after leaving Cannóbio.

ASCONA

Isadora Duncan, Herman Hesse and Paul Klee all spent time here, as did Lenin and Jung. The town's lakefront is traffic-free, allowing visitors to savour it in peace. Ascona is separated from the larger, better-known town of Locarno by the wide Maggia river. Those with time to spare can follow the Valle Maggia to reach Ponte Brolla – the starting point of the enchantingly named Val Centovalli or the Valley of a Hundred Valleys which is fine walking country.

🔢 134 A4 ✉ Close to Locarno 🚌 Regular buses from Locarno 🚢 Regular lake steamers

LOCARNO

Locarno wraps itself around a sheltered inlet of the lake which, because it faces southwest and the lower hills, gets many hours of sunlight. The lakefront and nearby squares are alive with bright flowers and pleasant outdoor cafés. Inland from the lake, past the Kursaal Casino, the **Castello Visconti** is now a museum of local archaeology. At the heart of the old town is Piazza Grande, with its shops and restaurants. If you head north from it, along Via della Stazione, you will come across the lower station of a *funivia* (cable car). This leads to the 15th-century church of Madonna del Sasso with superb views of the lake and the cablecar, then a chairlift that rises to 1,672m (5,485ft). Elsewhere in the town, the Casa Rusca in Piazza Sant'Antonio, a fine 17th-century house, has a tradition of being occupied by artists, and holds regular exhibitions of work by contemporary painters and sculptors.

🔢 134 A4

Castello Visconti

✉ Locarno ☎ 091 7563461 🕐 Apr–Oct Tue–Sun 10–12, 2–5
✋ Moderate 🍴 Villa Pauliska (€€), Via Orselina 6; 091 7430541

Lake Orta

By comparison to the lakes to the east, Orta is just a splash of water, yet at 14km (9 miles) long, 3km (2 miles) wide and 143m (470ft) deep it would be a large lake in other locations.
✚ 134 D2

ISOLA SAN GIÚLIO

Visitors staying in Orta San Giúlio (► 30–31) who rise with the sun and look out across the lake are sometimes treated to a rare sight. A thin, dense layer of mist lies on the water, waiting for just a little more sunlight before it rises and disperses, and above it, seemingly floating on a cloud, is Isola San Giulio. A similar, more easily observed but less striking view can be seen each night

when buildings on the island are floodlit and seem disembodied against the dark waters of the lake and the mountains beyond.

On the island, the church dedicated to the founding saint is the finest Romanesque building in the area. Built in the 9th century on the site of San Giuilo's hermit cell, it contains many treasures. The black marble pulpit is 11th century, the carved lecterns and walnut choir stalls are masterpieces and a silver urn holds the remains of Giúlio himself. A section of bone from one of the dragons the saint displaced is probably whalebone. Beside the church the 14th-century Palazzo dei Viscovi is now a monastery.

🚌 134 D2 ✉ Island off Orta San Giúlio at the southern end of Lake Orta
🍴 Limited on the island, but lots of choice in Orta San Giúlio (€–€€€)
🚢 Reached by regular lake steamers or water 'taxis' from Orta San Giulio

MADONNA DEL SASSO AND LAKE ORTA'S WESTERN SHORE

Lake Orta's western shore is steep, the road which links the hillside villages narrow and twisting. But there are worthwhile places to visit. The highlight is the church of Madonna del Sasso perched on a granite outcrop close to the village of Boleto. The church has some interesting artwork, including fine 18th-century frescoes and a 17th-century crucifix, but is most notable for the view from it which takes in virtually the entire lake.

Closer to Omegna are the upper and lower Quarna villages (Quarna Sopra and Quarno Sotto). The villages have a history of producing fine work in wood and brass and are particularly famous for making musical instruments. There is a small **museum of instruments** and their factory in Quarna Sotto, which is open during the summer months.

🚌 134 D1

Museum of Musical Instruments
✉ Quarna Sotto ☎ 0323 826368 🕐 Jul–Sep daily 10–12, 3–7
🖐 Inexpensive 🍴 Little locally, but a reasonable choice in Omegna
🚌 Infrequent buses from Omegna

OMEGNA

With a population of about 16,000, Omegna is Lake Orta's largest town. It is a pleasant place still retaining part of its 13th-century wall, though it is more industrialized than most of the other places on the lake. The ruins of an ancient bridge across the river still provoke debate between those experts who date its origins to the time when the town was Roman Vomenia, and those who detect more recent (but still medieval) work. Close to the lakefront is the town's old quarter, with some beautiful old houses, many still with

their outside stairways and wrought ironwork, with balconies and shutters. Be sure to find time to visit the church of Sant'Ambrogio, which has an excellent 16th-century polyptych.

✚ 134 C2 ✉ At the northern end of Lake Orta, straddling the lake's outflowing river 🍴 La Conchiglia (€€), Via IV Novembre 187; 032 362317 🚌 Buses from Gozzano and Gravellona Toce 🚢 Regular lake steamers

ORTA SAN GIÚLIO
Best places to see, ➤ 30–31.

Lake Como & the Bergamo Valleys

A glacier once filled the valleys that now carry the Adda and Mera rivers. It flowed south, bumping against the area of rock that underlies the High Brianza, its tip at the Punta Spartivento (near Bellagio).

Lago di Como

Bergamo

The rock of the triangle was hard, splitting the glacier and deepening two valleys to create a lake which is an inverted Y, the points of its arms at Como and Lecco. Interestingly, the Lecco arm lies a little higher than the Como arm so that the lake flows through the Adda, which flows past Lecco. There is no outlet on the Como arm and when rain increases the lake's volume beyond that which can be easily taken by the Adda the lake overflows, occasionally flooding Piazza Cavour, the lakeside square in Como.

Lake Como

Without doubt this is the most elegant of the lakes. Renowned for its gentle winter climate, Lake Como became the favourite destination of Europe's nobility and super-rich during the 19th century. Some who came were so enchanted they built villas, sumptious buildings set among gardens which were lovingly landscaped, the plants thriving in an ideal climate which offered abundant sun, adequate water and an absence of frosts and harsh cold. These villas and gardens set a tone which has never been eroded by mass tourism. Lake Como is a place for those who value peace and tranquillity.

➕ 136 A2

ARGEGNO

Argegno is a pretty town, best seen from the road which descends from the Intelvi villages, when the red-tiled roofs of the houses stand out against the wooded valley of the Telo river and the lake. The view from the lakefront is superb, with a long arm of the lake in both directions and, northwards, the mountains above Varenna, snow-capped in winter. To make the best of the view, go just a little out of town to the north and take the *funivia* to Pigra, well known not only as scenic overlook but for the profusion of wildflowers that grow near the top station.

➕ 136 B1 ✉ Lake Como's western shore 🍴 La Griglia (€), 1 Fraz Sant'Anna; 031 821147 🚌 Regular buses from Como ⛴ Regular lake steamers

BELLÁGIO

Best places to see, ➤ 22–23.

BELLANO

On the lake front of Bellano there are memorials to the 19th-century writer Tommaso Grossi and the 17th-century scientist Sigismondo Boldoni. Neither of the pair is very well known outside Italy, but Bellano is proud of its famous sons. It is also proud of the

fact that it was another member of the Boldoni family, Pietro, who introduced the silk Industry to Como.

The old quarter of the town is extremely attractive, but most visitors come to see the *orrido,* the gorge of the Pioverna stream, which is arguably the finest of its kind in the lakes' area. In spring melting snow swells the stream, the over the centuries extra volume has cut a deep narrow gorge through the rocks above the town. A series of ladders and walkways allows you to explore the gorge. When the stream level is high the spray and constant hammering of the water make this is an exciting journey.

➕ 136 A2 ✉ On Lake Como's eastern shore 🍴 La Darsena (€€), Via Alberto 8; 0341 810317 🚌 Regular buses along the eastern shore from Lecco 🚢 Regular lake steamers

CADENABBIA

Visitors heading north along the western shore of Lake Como beyond Argegno reach Sala Comacina and the start of the Zocca dell'Oli, the Olive Hollow (so named for the huge number of olive groves in the area). Beyond Ospedaletto's famous campanile are Tremezzo and Villa Carlotta (➤ 40–41), then Cadenabbia. The lake

is at its widest just beyond Bellagio's Punta Spartivento. The wideness of the lake minimizes the shading of the Grigna and the peaks of the High Brianza and explains the array of fine villas in and above the village. Verdi stayed in one while finishing his score for *La Traviata*. The village's position also explains why it is a terminus for Como's main car ferry, linking Cadenabbia with Bellagio and Varenna.

🕆 136 B2 ✉ Lake Como's western shore 🍴 The best locally is La Fagurida (€) in Rogaro Ovest near the village; 0344 40676 🚌 Regular buses along the lake's western shore 🚢 Regular lake steamers and car ferries link to Varenna and Bellagio

CERNOBBIO

Cernobbio is a small industrial town, though it has a fine old quarter and an excellent lakefront. At the northern edge of the town is Villa d'Este, built in the 16th century for Cardinal Tolomeo Gallio, Secretary of State to Pope Gregory XIII. No expense was spared, and it's claimed that the villa today looks much as it did when the cardinal took possession of it. Over the years the villa has been visited by some of the richest and most powerful of Europe's elite. It was named by Caroline, estranged wife of George Frederick, later King George IV of Britain. Believing herself to be descended from the Este family of Ferrara, Caroline altered the villa's name. The villa's gardens include a curious stepped double waterfall which flows across a bridge over the lakeside road from Cernobbio to Moltrasio, and a series of castellated lookouts carved into the rock face. Today, the villa is a luxury hotel that boasts a floating swimming pool, unique in Italy.

🕆 136 C1 ✉ On Lake Como's western shore 🍴 Harry's Bar (€), Piazza Risorgimento 2; 031 308080 🚌 Infrequent buses along the western shore from Como 🚢 Regular lake steamers

COMO

Como occupies an ancient site that has been inhabited since at least the Bronze Age. During the Roman period Julius Caesar himself brought 5,000 Greeks to settle in the town, the start of its rise to prosperity. After the fall of Rome, Como was the home of the Maestri Comacina, a group of architects, builders and sculptors whose work is still admired today. The disastrous Ten Years War (1118–1127) with Milan ruined the town, but it eventually recovered and became noted for its wool and silk industries, and today Como is still the heart of Italian silk production.

 136 C1

Broletto

Piazza Duomo lies just a few steps inland from Piazza Cavour and the lake. As you enter the square, the first building on your left is the Broletto, the 13th-century town hall. It has an arcaded ground floor with triple-arched windows above, and is attached to a tall campanile.

✉ Piazza Duomo

Duomo

Dominating Piazza Duomo is the west façade of the cathedral, a masterpiece of Gothic architecture with statues peering out from its niches. The façade dates from the 15th century, but the Duomo took many years to complete and shows a range of styles. The eastern end mixes Gothic and Renaissance and the dome was added only in the 18th century. The oldest section of the building was the work of the Rodari brothers and it was they who carved the exquisite south door and the Porta della Rana, the Frog door, on the north side, so called because there is a frog carved on one pillar. Inside, the Duomo has some good artwork, including paintings by Bernardino Luini.

🍽 Piazza Duomo L'Imbarcadero (€€€), Piazza Cavour 20; 031 270166. La Colonne (€€), Piazza Mazzini 12; 031 266166

Porta Vittoria

At the far end of the old town from the lake is a tall, sturdy tower
built in the 12th century to protect one of the gates through the
old wall. During the wars of the Risorgimento Garibaldi defeated
an Austrian army under Marshall Urban at nearby San Fermo and
marched in triumph through Porta Vittoria.

✉ Via Cantú/Piazza Vittoria

Sant'Abbondio and San Carpoforo

These two fine basilicas, both the work of the Maestri Comacina,
are named after early Christians who preached in the Como area.
With its severe façade and twin towers, Sant'Abbondio is now
recognized as one of the great masterpieces of the Lombard
Romanesque style. Inside, it has rows of elegant columns and
superb 14th-century frescoes which illustrate the life of Christ.

San Carpoforo is thought to occupy the site of a Roman temple
to Mercury, but has a Christian tradition which is at least 1,500
years long. The exterior is similar to that of Sant'Abbondio, but
inside it is a complete contrast, with elegant steps and
unfrescoed walls.

Sant'Abbondio
✉ Via Sant'Abbondio
San Carpoforo
✉ Via Brenta

San Fedele

San Fedele is probably the finest of Como's trio of churches
built by the Maestri Comacina. Found in Piazza San Fedele, in
the middle of the old town, this wonderful building contains
breathtaking frescoes dating from the 14th to the 16th centuries.
Take time however to enjoy it's exterior with a stroll around
the square.

✉ Piazza San Fedele

GRAVEDONA

Gravedona is a good base for exploring the northern section of Lake Como's western shore. In medieval times the town was the senior partner of the Tre Pievi – the Three Parishes, the other two being Dongo and Sorico – which maintained its independence of the city states to the south. The Tre Pievi occasionally supplemented trade with piracy, using a ship with a golden crucifix attached to the prow, which the villagers claimed made it invincible. Once the ship attacked and defeated a treasure ship of the Emperor Frederick I (the feared Barbarossa – 'Red Beard'). The Emperor was outraged, but the gold was to support his campaign against the Lombard League and after his defeat at the battle of Legnano in 1176 he was forced to make concessions in the Treaty of Constance in 1183. Some of those concessions were to the Tre Pievi.

Gravedona has some fine buildings.

The town council now occupies the 'Villa of Delights' of Cardinal Tolomeo Gallio (who also owned Villa d'Este at Cernobbio ➤ 93), while the 12th-century church of Santa Maria del Tiglio, which was built on the site of a 5th-century baptistery, still shows sections of the mosaic flooring of the original. Dongo, a little way south of Gravedona, had entered history as the site of Mussolini's death, which is unfortunate, because that infamous period can distract from the village's picturesque position and very pretty old centre.

The northwestern section of Lake Como is famous for its reliable winds and has become a favourite with sailors and water sport enthusiasts. Pianello del Lario, south of Gravedona, is the home of the lake's most important sailing club, while to the north, the pretty village of Domaso is renowned as the best place on Lake Como for windsurfing.

135 B7 Lauro (€), Via Tagliaferri 12, Gravedona; 034 485255. Spinnaker (€), Via Calozzo, Pianello del Lario; 0344 87219 Regular buses along the western shore Regular lake steamers

LECCO

There is a good deal of rivalry between Lecco and Como. The cities are about equal in size, and while Como is more historically interesting (and, most unbiased observers would maintain, more elegant), Lecco is without doubt more dramatically located, beside the lake's only outflow river and below the steep cliffs of Monte Coltignone to the northwest, and the Resegone to the east. Though the Como arm of the lake and its single northern reach are part of Lake Como, it would be a brave person who would not refer to the eastern arm as Lake Lecco when staying in the town.

Piani d'Erna is a popular walking area beneath the Resegone; you get there by a cable car from Versasio above the town, which offers a splendid view of Lecco and the lake.

The town lies entirely on the lake's eastern shore and is reached from the west by two bridges that span the Adda. The farthest of these from the lake is Ponte Visconti, built on the orders of Azzone Visconti in 1336. The original bridge had drawbridge sections at each end. When it was renovated to look as it had when originally built, its 11 arches were maintained, but plans stopped short of reproducing the drawbridges. In Piazza XX Septembre, the Torre Visconti is another reminder of Milanese influence. A market has been held in the square below the tower since at least 1149. Elsewhere, there is a fine statue of Lecco's famous writer, Alessandro Manzoni (1785–1873); his childhood home is now a **museum** with a collection of memorabilia. The town's tourist office also produces a leaflet identifying places mentioned in Manzoni's book *The Betrothed*. Most of the sites are actually in Olate, a village above and east of the town. To the north of Villa Manzoni, and also worth visiting, is **Palazzo Belgioioso,** a 17th-century mansion which now houses the town's museum.

✚ 136 C3 ✉ At the southern tip of Lake Como's eastern arm 🚌 Regular buses from Como 🚢 Regular lake steamers 🍴 Cermenati (€€), Corso Matteotti 71; 0341 283017

Manzoni Museum

✉ Via Guonella 7 ☎ 0341 481247 🕐 Tue–Sun 9:30–2 ✋ Moderate

Palazzo Belgioioso

✉ Corso Matteotti 32 ☎ 0341 481247 🕐 Tue–Sun 9:30–2 ✋ Moderate
🚌 Regular buses from Como

MENÁGGIO

Menággio's position, halfway along the western shore of Lake Como, where an easy route links the Como valley to the Lugano valley and Switzerland, means that the town has always been an important trading centre. As always, trade brings traffic, but away from this the town is well worth the visit. During the Ten Years War of the 12th century, Menággio chose the wrong side and was destroyed. It was a mistake the townsfolk made again several times in medieval times; they also picked fights with the Spanish and the Austrians during their periods of dominance.

The town has a very good beach – something of a rarity on Lake Como – and one of the most romantically sited golf courses in Italy. It is also a good base for exploring both the Val Menággio and the hills to the northwest. The Val Menággio road passes the little lake of Piano, once part of Lake Lugano but separated from it by a landslide. The lake is now part of a nature reserve.

From Menággio the minor road to Pièsio and Breglia passes through Loveno, a village that is almost unchanged since early medieval times. From Breglia, a good walk climbs Monte Grona, with views of both Lake Como and Lake Lugano, while a longer walk follows the upper parts of Valle Sanagra to Monte Bregagno and an even wider panorama.

➕ 136 A2 🍴 Lario (€€), Via IV Novembre 12; 0344 32368 🚌 Regular buses from Como and Porlezza 🚢 Regular lake steamers; car ferries from Varenna/Bellagio

PIONA

At the northern end of Lake Como's eastern shore, two spits of land almost touch, creating the sheltered bay of Laghetto di Piona, the little Piona lake. At the point of the western headland sits the **Piona Abbey.** It is likely that this site was an ancient and holy one even before the Christian era, and there was certainly a Christian church before the abbey was founded by the Cluniac monks in 1138. Early in the 20th century the abbey was taken over by Cistercians. The monks distil liqueurs including Gocce Imperiali whch has a reputation for being really potent. Parts of the abbey are open to visitors. The church is the oldest section but the mid-13th-century cloisters, a lovely mix of Gothic and Renaissance styles, are the most interesting. Outside the abbey the small garden offers wonderful views across the lake to Gravedona.

North of Lake Piona is Colico, built at the edge of the marshland of Piano di Spagna, famous for its wildlife and migrating birds. Close to the Valtellina, the valley of the Adda and the Spluga Pass, the town was by turns prosperous on trade and subject to attacks by bandits. South of the abbey, Corenno Plinio is a pretty village named after Pliny the Elder, who loved this section of the lake. Just beyond is Dervio, filling a rounded headland where the lake is at its narrowest. The strategic importance of this is reflected in the sparse ruins of medieval fortifications.

➕ 136 A3 ✉ At the northern end of Lake Como's eastern shore 🍴 Albergo Ristorante Belvedere (€€), Via Olgiasca 53, Colico; 0341 940330 🚢 Regular lake steamers from Colico

Piona Abbey

☎ 0341 940331 🕐 Daily 9–12, 2–6 🎫 Free

VARENNA

The houses of Varenna have been built on a steep hill on top of which sit the ruins of a castle (Castello Vezio), which was the last home of Theodolinda, a 7th-century Lombard queen. The castle controlled the lake at the point where it divides and, situated on its outcrop of the Grigna, was virtually impregnable. The castle gave the village that grew up around it a certain prosperity, which was enhanced when the survivors of Como's destruction of Isola Comacina made their homes here and opened a quarry for the black marble found in outcrops near the town. The marble quarry kept the town prosperous for many years. By contrast, the product of a later son of the town did nothing for the local economy.

G. B. Pirelli was born in Varenna, but his tire empire did not include a Varenna factory. The Pirelli calendars were never produced here either.

Besides the array of fine old houses, Varenna boasts two superb villas. Villa Cipressi (currently closed to the public) on Via IV Novembre has terraced gardens going down to the lake edge and lovely views across the water. To the south of the town, **Villa Monastero** is even more impressive, both for its building and its grounds. The villa was constructed in 1208 for Cistercian nuns but in the 16th century the sisters acquired a reputation for conduct distinctly unchaste and the convent was closed on the orders of San Carlo Borromeo. The villa passed into private hands and was then acquired by the Italian government. It is now used as a summer school for the sciences. It is a beautiful building with a stone staircase rising from the lake, lovely arched windows and an arcaded terrace. The grounds are equally attractive, with fine shrubbery and masses of citrus trees.

Back in the village, birdwatchers will want to visit the **ornithological museum,** where all the species which have been seen on the lake are displayed.

➕ 136 B2 ✉ Eastern shore 🍴 Vecchia Varenna (€€), Contrada Scoscesa 10; 0341 830793 🚌 Regular buses from Lecco 🚢 Regular lake steamers and car ferries

Villa Monastero

☎ 0341 830129 🕐 May–Oct 10–12:30, 2:30–6
✋ Moderate

Museo Civico Ornitologico

☎ 0341 830119 🕐 Jun to mid-Sep Mon–Fri 10–12, 3:30–6; Sat and Sun 10–12; mid-Sep to May Thu and Sat 3–5
✋ Inexpensive

VILLA CARLOTTA
Best places to see, ➤ 40–41.

What to see in the Bergamo Valleys

The relatively unknown city of Bergamo has
a long history and a beautifully preserved
medieval heart. North of Bergamo two valleys,
each with numerous branches, head back
towards the mountains which form the
southern ridge of the Valtellina.

BERGAMO

Bergamo is two cities, the modern lower
one and the medieval upper one (Città Alta).
Though the main attractions are concentrated
in the Città Alta, visitors should not ignore the
lower city. The monument to Bergamo-born
composer Donizetti (1797–1848) is in Piazza
Cavour, while the theatre named after him
stands on the Sentierone, which links
Piazza Cavour to Piazza Vittorio Veneto. The
composer's birthplace and a **museum** to
him can be visited in the upper city. The
lower city also has two fine churches: San
Bartolomeo, with frescoes by Lorenzo Lotto,
and Sant'Alessandro in Colonna. The column
outside the latter church marks the reputed
spot where the saint was martyred in AD 297. If
you head up to the upper city by road rather
than *funivia,* you will pass the **Accademia
Carrara,** which has many fine paintings.

The focus in the upper city, is the Piazza
Vecchia (Best places to see, ► 32–33), but
there is much else to see. In Piazza del Duomo
stands the cathedral, dating from the mid-15th
century (though the dome and façade are 19th
century). Beside the cathedral is the basilica of

Santa Maria Maggiore, a 12th-century building with a superb porch in red and white marble and a sumptuous interior. Built into the side of the basilica is the **Colleoni Chapel,** built by Bartolomeo Colleoni, a *condottiere* (mercenary soldier) who twice captained Venetian forces against Milan and twice led the Milanese against Venice, growing rich in the process. Colleoni constructed the chapel as his mausoleum: He died in 1476 just after the chapel was finished.

✚ 136 D4

Museo Donizettiano

✉ 9 Via Arena, Upper City ☎ 035 399269 ◷ Jun–Sep Tue–Sun 9:30–1, 2–5:30 ✋ Inexpensive

Accademia Carrara

✉ Piazza dell'Accademia 82A ☎ 035 399643 ◷ Apr–Sep Tue–Sun 10–1, 3–6:45; Oct–Mar Tue–Sun 9:30–1, 2:30–5:45 ✋ Moderate, Sun free

Santa Maria Maggiore

✉ Piazza del Duomo ☎ 035 223327/246855 ◷ Daily 9–12:30, 2–6:30 (4:30 from Nov–Feb) ✋ Free

Colleoni Chapel

✉ Piazza del Duomo ☎ 035 210061 ✋ Free

VAL BREMBANA

Brembana is the westerly of the two valleys. The Brembo River's geography meant that until the 17th century only two difficult passes allowed entry into the valley, the isolation allowing the local people to evolve a rich folklore, including their own dialect and architectural style. At Almenno San Bartolomeo, the **Museo del Falegname** is devoted to the local craft of woodworking. At Sedrina a picturesque series of bridges crosses the river. The rock here is limestone and has been eaten away by rain and river water to form caves. One, the **Grotte delle Meraviglie,** can be visited. Farther on there is a good **museum of the valley** in Zogno. San Pellegrino Terme is the best-known village in the valley. Once one of the leading spas in Lombardy, it is now famous for its mineral water, which can be found across Italy. Beyond San Pellegrino there are enough small villages and remote side valleys to keep the visitor entertained for several days. At the head of the valley, Foppolo is the best developed ski resort in the area.

✚ 136 C4

Museo del Falegname

✉ Via Aldo Mero 6, Almenno San Bartolomeo
☎ 035 549198/544411 🕐 Sat 3–6, Sun 9:30–12, 3–6
✋ Inexpensive 🍽 Palanca (€), Via Dogana 15; 035 640800

Grotte delle Meraviglie

✉ Sedrina ☎ 0345 91044/55007 🕐 May–Sep some Sun 2:30–6. Check dates with Tourist Office
✋ Inexpensive 🍽 Opportunities locally. In San Pellegrino Terme Tirolese (€), Via De Medici 3; 0345 22267

Museo della Valle

✉ Zogno ☎ 0345 91473 ⏰ Tue–Sun 9–12, 2–5 ✋ Inexpensive

VAL SERIANA

The lower reaches of the Serio river valley are industrialized, but the upper valley remains unspoiled. Abbazia is named after its 12th-century Cistercian abbey, a delightful building. Farther on is Gandino with a medieval gateway and a fine 15th-century basilica with a baroque interior. From the village a chairlift takes visitors to a plateau that is a ski resort in winter and offers good walking in summer. Farther on is Vertova, where the church is surrounded by an arcade that makes it look like a hen protecting her chicks. There is an even more impressive church at Clusone. The Oratorio dei Disciplini has frescoes that include a 'Dance of Death', people and skeletons hand in hand. The final village in the valley is Valbondione, from which a walk leads to the Cascata del Serio, reputedly Europe's highest waterfall at 315m (1,033ft). Sadly the stream which feeds it is now diverted into a hydroelectric station, the waterfall only being 'turned on' during certain summer weekends.

✚ 137 C5

Eastern Lakes

Lago
d' Iseo

Lago d' Garda

Bréscia
☐

Verona
☐

**Well removed
from the
collection of lakes in
the west of Lombardy and
Piedmont lie two more large lakes and
a number of smaller ones. The way that these eastern
lakes came into existence was, of course, similar –
though there is a subtle difference which we will
explore when reaching Lake Garda. There is, however,
a slight change in climate, the lakes lying farther from**

**the mountains, and,
particularly on Lake
Garda, there are
more beaches.**

The choice of beach have
made Iseo and Garda
centres for sun-seeking
tourists. However, this does
not mean that there is any
shortage of interesting
historical sites, beautiful
villas and gardens, or walks to be enjoyed on high ridges. There
are wonderful towns to visit – Bréscia, with its Roman remains,
Romeo and Juliet's Verona and the incomparable Venice. But
there are also more places geared mainly towards entertainment
and pleasure.

BRÉSCIA

Bréscia is Lombardy's second
city, with a population of about
200,000. It stands at the
mouth of the Val Trompia, which
descends from the pre-Alps of
Lombardy's northern border.
The city has some of Italy's
best Roman remains as
well as excellent medieval
buildings.

✠ 138 E3

Colle Cidneo

The oldest part of the city is the
hilltop of Colle Cidneo, where
there are Roman remains, the
ruins of a 5th-century church
and the 14th-century Visconti
castle. In the castle is a
Risorgimento museum and
an **arms museum.**

Risorgimento Museum
✉ Colle Cidneo ☎ 030 44176
🕓 Jun–Sep Tue–Sun 10–5;
Oct–May Tue–Sun 9:30–1, 2:30–5
✋ Moderate 🍴 La Sosta (€€€), Via
San Martino della Battaglia 20; 030
295603

Arms Museum
✉ Colle Cidneo ☎ 030 293292
🕓 Jun–Sep Tue–Sun 10–5;
Oct–May Tue–Sun 9:30–1, 2:30–5
✋ Moderate

Piazza Duomo

There are two cathedrals here, the older one (Duomo Vecchia or Rotonda) dating from the 11th century. It has a severe look, but an unusual circular design, and some remarkable treasures, including a sliver of the True Cross and a Holy Thorn. The newer cathedral is 16th-century baroque, but with a much newer dome. North of the cathedrals is the 13th-century Broletto and the Torre del Popolo, the people's tower.

Piazza Loggia

The Loggia replaced the Broletto as the town hall after it was constructed in the 15th century and still retains that function. The lower floor of the building was designed by Bramante, while the upper floor was by Palladio – a remarkable pedigree. Opposite the Loggia is the Palazzo dell'Orologio, topped by two Venetian figures in distinctly Moorish style. The picturesque older quarter of the city lies close to the piazza.

Via dei Musei

Bréscia's real treasures lie on this street. Here stand the ruins of the Capitoline Temple and those of a theatre from the 1st-century AD, which itself stood at the edge of the forum. Farther along the road is the **Museo della Città,** housed in the 16th-century monastery of San Giulio, though the site also has the remains of an 8th-century Benedictine nunnery and a 9th-century basilica. The complex houses collections, which, until very recently, formed the town's Roman and Christian museums. The Roman treasures include such objects as a 1st-century bronze Winged Victory and six bronze busts of 2nd- and 3rd-century emperors. The Christian collection has many priceless items, the best of which include the

Lipsanoteca, a 4th-century ivory reliquary and the 8th-century jewel-encrusted Cross of Desiderius.

Museo della Città

✉ Via dei Musei 81B ☎ 030 2777833 🕐 Jun–Sep Tue–Sun 10–6; Oct–May Tue–Sun 9:30–5:30 ✋ Moderate

Val Sabbia and Lake Idro

East of Bréscia, about halfway between the city and Lake Garda, the N45 road heads north, soon reaching the Chiese river. Geography prevents the Chiese from flowing into the lake, though it seems to want to, bypassing it by just 3km (2 miles) at Salò. From that point, near Tormini, the N237 follows the river closely as it flows through the Val Sabbia near a series of pretty villages. At Sabbio Chiese, the old castle on a large rock outcrop has been transformed into two churches, one on top of the other. Beyond Sabbio Chiese, the valley narrows, the church at Barghe seeming to grow out of the rock. Continue through Vestone, from where roads lead off into the mountains, to reach Lake Idro.

Idro is the highest lake in Lombardy, lying 368m (1,207ft) above sea level. It is 11km (7 miles) long and up to 2km (1.25 miles) wide. In places, especially on the northwestern shore, the surrounding mountains fall so steeply into the water that from the opposite shore they seem to rise vertically. Idro, the lake's largest village, lies just off the main road. It is a tourist village and here, and at nearby Crone and Vantone, the campsites fill rapidly in summer. There are more campsites on the western shore, especially near Anfo, where there is a Venetian-built castle on the Rocca d'Anfo. Beyond Anfo a road winds towards the mountains, through Bagolino, a pretty village of narrow streets. Back on the shore road, the visitor reaches Ponte Caffaro, the last village of Val Sabbia.

🍴 Alpino (€€), Crone, Via Lungolago 20, near Idro; 0365 823378

🚌 Regular buses from Bréscia and Desenzano del Garda

What to see around Lake Garda

Lake Garda is best known as a vacation spot, with a string of campsites along its eastern shore and many more on the shore line north of Desenzano. But it has other fine features too – the historical towns of Sirmione and Malcésine, good walking areas in Tignale, Tremosine and Monte Baldo, and excellent restaurants that serve food to enjoy with a glass of local wine.

✚ 139 D6

DESENZANO DEL GARDA

Desenzano is the most important town on the southern lake, with a railway station on the Milan–Venice line and its own exit from the A4 autostrada. The site has been important for centuries. The

Romans built a fort here on the Capo la Terra, the highest part of the present town. In medieval times a castle was built on the remains of the Roman works. Roman Desenzano is also evident at **Villa Romana,** the excavated remains of a 3rd- or 4th-century villa. The prize exhibit in what is considered the most important Roman villa in northern Italy is more than 200sq m (240sq yards) of mosaic, depicting hunting and everyday life scenes. There is a small museum where the best of the excavated finds are displayed. The town also has a **museum** exploring the pre-Roman history of the area. The 16th-century Duomo is also worth visiting to see *The Last Supper* of the Venetian painter Tiepolo.

Desenzano has a very picturesque old harbour, its edges dotted with trees and an array of fine buildings. A good local market is held close to and around the harbour on Tuesdays. In the evening the old harbour is perfect for a romantic stroll.

Close to Desenzano the village of Padenghe sul Garda is worth visiting. Houses here have been built within the walls of an old castle, giving it a medieval feel.

✚ 139 F5 ⑪ Caffé Italia (€€), Piazza Malvezzi 19; 030 9141243 🚍 Regular buses from local towns and villages ⛴ Desenzano is the headquarters and terminus of the Garda lake steamers 🚆 Train station on the line from Milan to Venice

Villa Romana
✉ Via Crocefisso 22 🕓 Mar to mid-Oct Tue–Fri 8:30–7, Sat and Sun 9–5:30; mid-Oct to Feb Tue–Fri 8:30–4:30, Sat and Sun 9–4:30 ☎ 030 9143547 🖐 Moderate

Museo Civico Archeologico
✉ Via Anelli 22 🕓 Tue and Fri–Sun 3–7 ☎ 030 9144529 🖐 Moderate

GARDA

The town named after the lake stands below Monte Garda, a natural fortress topped by the remnants of several castles, the last built by the Scaligeri. Under Scaligeri rule the town's Palazzo dei Capitano was also built, though the name derives from the time of Venetian rule, when the building housed the Serenissima's Captain of the Lake, the local official. A much more impressive building is the Villa Albertini, a romantic, castle-like villa where the treaty was signed which united Piedmont and Lombardy, which many historians date as the start of the Risorgimento. More local history is on display at the **museum of Torri del Benaco** (housed in the remains of yet another Scaligeri castle), the next village along the eastern shore. This museum also includes several examples of the prehistoric rock engravings found on Monte Luppia and at Punta San Vigilio, both close to Garda. You should visit the Punta itself – though surviving examples of the rock carvings are extremely difficult to find. It is one of the most beautiful places on the lake, with tremendous views across to Manerba and the Salò bay. At the tip is a dignified little church – it has a niche statue which is only visible from the water.

Torri del Benaco lies to the north of Garda – it is linked to Maderno by Lake Garda's only car ferry – while to the south is Bardolino, famous for its red wine produced from the vineyards covering the hillside above the town.

✚ 139 E6 🍴 Trattoria Da Pino (€€), Via Poiano 5; 045 7255694 🚌 Regular buses along the eastern lake shore 🚢 Regular lake steamers

Museo Castello Scaligero (Tower Museum)

✉ Torri del Benaco 🕓 Apr–Oct daily 9:30–12:30, 2:30–6; Nov Sat and Sun 9:30–12:30, 2:30–6 ☎ 045 6296111 🚌 Regular buses along the eastern lake shore

LAZISE

Lazise has another of Garda's Scaligeri castles, almost as impressive as the one at Sirmione, though not as well positioned. The castle is now a private house and cannot be visited. In former times, a chain could be drawn from the castle across the harbour mouth to provide a protective 'wall'. When Lake Garda formed part of the Venetian Republic, a fleet of warships was maintained here, an amazing fact given the size of the harbour, which seems far too small to have fulfilled such a role. The

Venetians referred to Lazise as the 'Key to Lake Garda' because the fleet controlled the southern lake. Today the warships are long gone, the harbour occupied only by a few fishing boats and pleasure craft. Around the harbour are a number of small hotels and cafés that are guaranteed to make any stay in the town a delight. As well as the castle, the town also has sections of the equally impressive arched medieval town wall complete with fishtail embattlements.

✚ 139 E6 ✉ On the eastern shore of Lake Garda 🍴 Alla Grotta (€€); 045 7580035

LIMONE SUL GARDA

Most people assume that the village was named after the lemon trees which, some believe, were grown here for the first time in Europe and made the early village prosperous. Some others claim the lemon story is a legend and that the village is actually named after a son of the god Benacus. The lemon story is certainly supported by the bushes which now grow in profusion, as do orange and mandarin trees. A new road, the Gardesana Occidentale, now speeds visitors along Garda's western shore, bypassing Limone, which has, thankfully, become a quiet place again as a result. The discerning can stroll in peace, delighting in the houses of the old quarter with their balconies and flower boxes, and the village's setting below dazzling white cliffs. Amid such beauty, the inscription on the external wall of the church of San Pietro set in an olive grove on a hill close to the village comes as a shock. It tells of plague in 1630, a poor olive harvest in 1822 and the cruel winter of 1857, leading to an exodus from the village.

🚩 139 C6 ✉ On the western shore of Lake Garda 🍴 Bellavista (€), Lungolago Marconi; 036 5954522 🚌 Regular buses along the western lake shore ⛴ Regular lake steamers

MALCÉSINE

Some visitors would argue that Malcésine deserves a place in the 'Top Ten' of the lakes area, and, after Sirmione, it is probably the most delightful of all Garda's villages. Certainly, the view of the castle from the beach and several picturesque parts of the old village make a trip to the town a must. The section of Garda's eastern shore that lies in Veneto is occasionally called the Riviera of Olives, and Malcésine is the area's undisputed capital. The **castle**, built in the 14th century, remains almost complete and now houses the **Museo Pariani,** a museum of the lake, with exhibits including information on the towing of war galleys to Torbole (➤ 125).

Within the town any walk will be worthwhile. **The Palazzo dei Capitani,** the headquarters of the Venetian lake captains (officials), near the harbour is the most impressive building, but there are many other exquisite houses, some reached along narrow arcaded streets. On the north side of the village is the lower station of the *funivia* to Monte Baldo.

✚ 139 C6 🍴 Trattoria Vecchia Malcésine (€), Via Pisort 6; 045 7400469 🚢 Regular lake steamers 🚌 Regular buses along the eastern lake shore

Castle/Museo Pariani

✉ On Lake Garda's eastern shore ☎ 045 7400837
🕐 Apr–Oct daily 9–7:30; Nov–Mar Sat and Sun 9–5
✋ Moderate

Palazzo dei Capitani

☎ 045 7400024/7400346 🕐 May–Sep daily 9–8
✋ Inexpensive

PESCHIERA DEL GARDA

Between Sirmione (➤ 36–37) and Peschiera the visitor crosses from Lombardy to Veneto, making Peschiera the first village of the Riviera of Olives. Because of its position, where the Mincio river leaves the lake, the site of Peschiera has always been important. The Romans had a town here, while the Lombards had a fishing village, and the Scaligeri built a castle and a walled harbour to defend the river crossing. The castle is mentioned by Dante in the *Divine Comedy*. It was destroyed by the Austrians but they reinforced the walls, making the village one of the corners of their 'defensive quadrilateral'. After the Austrians were defeated the walls were not needed, but were too massive to demolish.

West of Peschiera, visitors can see the sites of the two battles of 24 June 1859. On that day, a Piemontian army under Vittorio Emanuele II fought the right wing of the Austrian army close to a village now called San Martino della Battaglia, while a short distance to the south, at Solferino, the French under Napoleon III attacked the main Austrian army under Emperor Franz Josef. More than 40,000 men were killed or wounded, the defeated Austrians being allowed to retreat by the exhausted victors. Today, each of the sites has a commemorative tower (though the one at San Martino predates the battle) and an ossuary chapel. The Solferino tower houses a museum of the battle.

✚ 139 F6 ✉ At the eastern end of Lake Garda's southern shore 🍴 La Torretta (€€), Via G. Garibaldi 12; 045 7550108 🚌 Regular buses from Desenzano

RIVA DEL GARDA

Situated at the northern end of the lake, Riva is Garda's most famous holiday resort. The town handles this fame with grace, managing to maintain its character as a fishing/trading port even though the visitors outnumber the locals. The heart of the town is Piazza Tre Novembre, dominated by the Torre Apponale, a 13th-century clocktower, and the arched buildings of the old town hall.

Just a step away is the **moated castle** built to protect the town from pirates. The castle now houses a small **museum** of local history and an art gallery, and its irresistible approach – over a double-arched bridge and now fixed drawbridge – ensures a steady stream of visitors. Among other things, you can see objects from the prehistoric dwellings discovered beside Lake Ledro, the tiny lake to the west of Riva. From the town, you can drive to the top of Monte Brione or take the *funivia* for the short ride to the Bastione for tremendous views of the lake.

✚ 139 B7 ✉ At the northern tip of Lake Garda ⑪ Mediterraneo (€), Piazza Garibaldi 6; 0464 550175 🚍 Regular buses along both lake shores
🚢 Regular lake steamers

Castle/museum
☎ 0464 573869 ③ Apr–Oct Tue–Sun 10:30–6:30, also Mon mid-Jun to Sep
✋ Moderate

SALÒ

Salò is set at the farthest reach of an inlet of Lake Garda, an enviable position which shelters it from winds. The town has a fine 15th-century cathedral that houses some excellent artwork including a polyptych by Paolo Veneziano. Look for the equally attractive 16th-century Palazzo Municipale. On the first floor is a bust of Gasparo Bertolotti (known as Gasparo da Salò), who is usually credited with the invention of the violin.

North of Salò is Gardone Riviera. Here, be sure to visit the **Botanical Gardens,** first planted by Dr Arthur Hruska early in the 20th century and since taken over by the artist André Heller, who has added works combining art and ecology. Also worth visiting is **Il Vittoriale** (Vittoriale degli Italiani) an extraordinary complex constructed by Gabriele d'Annunzio, regarded as one of Italy's most flamboyant characters. He was a poet and soldier, and leader of the disastrous campaign to occupy Fiume (Rijeka) in 1919. In his will d'Annunzio left Il Vittoriale to the State. It is a collection of

buildings, many in art nouveau style, and an open air theatre. D'Annunzio's old house is much as he left it and visitors can also see his mausoleum, which is as extravagant as the man himself.

Beyond Gardone are the twin towns of Toscalano-Maderno, linked by Garda's only car ferry to Torri del Benaco, and Gargagno, where the Villa Fetrenelli was the seat of government of Mussolini's ill-fated Salò Republic.

✚ 139 D5 ✉ In a deep bay of Lake Garda's western shore 🍴 Villa Rimbalzello (€€), Via Trento 28; 0365 21069 🚌 Regular buses from Desenzano ⛴ Regular lake steamers

Giardino Botanico

✉ Via Roma, Gardone Riviera ☎ 0336 410877 🕐 Mid-Mar to mid-Oct 9–7 🚌 Regular buses ⛴ Regular lake steamers ✋ Moderate

Il Vittoriale

✉ Gardone Sopra ☎ 0365 296511 🕐 Park: daily 8:30–8 (9–5 from Oct–Mar). House: Apr–Sep Tue–Sun 9.30–7; Oct–Mar Tue–Sun 9–1, 2–5. War Museum: Apr–Sep Tue–Sun 10–6 ⛴ Regular lake steamers ✋ Expensive

SIRMIONE

Best places to see, ➤ 36–37.

TIGNALE/TREMÓSINE

Best places to see, ➤ 38–39.

TORBOLE

From a distance Torbole is a great sight with its fjord-like lake, the vast wedges of white rock falling into the water, and the many windsurfers who descend on the town each summer to exploit Garda's dependable winds dotting the lake. In Piazza Veneto, a plaque notes that Goethe set out from Torbole on the journey that ended with arrest at Malcésine, and it was here that Goethe began work on his Iphigenia.

✚ 139 B7 ✉ Northern tip of Lake Garda 🚌 Regular buses along both lake shores ⛴ Regular lake steamers

Lake Iseo

Lake Iseo is the fifth largest of the lakes, 24km (15 miles) long and
5km (3 miles) across at its widest. However, at that widest point
the lake is almost filled by Monte Isola, the largest island not only
on any of the lakes but on any lake in Europe.

🕂 138 C2

ISEO

Iseo has a 12th-century church that holds the remains of several
members of the Oldofredi family, local lords in medieval times.
One tomb is built into the façade. The Oldofredi were also
responsible for the castle that is now incorporated into the village
hall. The village's lakefront offers walks with fine views.

Iseo can be used as a base for exploring the southern part of
the lake. To the west is Sarnico, terminus for the lake steamers.
It is an interesting town with the remains of old fortifications,
echoes of its past as a fishing port and buildings designed by
Sommarciga, one of Italy's foremost art nouveau architects.
Between Iseo and Sarnico is Paratico, which has a ruined castle,
where it's claimed Dante stayed. Northeastward along the lake
from Iseo, Pilzone village is pleasantly set behind a headland.

🕂 138 D2 ✉ Southern shore of Lake Iseo 🍴 Il Paiolo (€€), Piazza Mazzini,
9; 030 9821074 🚌 Regular buses from Bréscia 🚢 Regular lake steamers

LÓVERE AND LAKE ISEO'S WESTERN SHORE

Before exploring the western shore take a detour from Pisogne to visit the historically important Val Camonica. On the valley rocks prehistoric humans have engraved and painted a tribal record extending from at least 5,000BC until the time of the Romans. The best of the work is in the vicinity of Capo di Ponte, where there is a museum on the engravings, and marked walks around the sites. The Archeodromo at Cenno has a reconstructed tribal village.

On the shore, Lóvere is the lake's main resort, but is also a town of great character and interest. There are the remains of medieval fortifications, including three surviving towers, and an art gallery housed in the beautiful 19th-century Palazzo Tadini. Beyond Lóvere are further geological marvels, the two *bögns* of Castro and Zorzino. The *bögns* are huge sheets of limestone that plunge steeply into the lake.

✚ 138 B2

Parco della Incisioni Rupestiri (National Rock Engravings Park)

✉ Capo di Ponte 🕓 Park: Tue–Sun 8–7:30 (4:30 from Oct–Apr) ☎ 0364 42140; Study Centre/Museum: Mon–Fri 9–4 ☎ 0364 42091 🖐 Moderate 🍴 Trocadero (€), Via Roma 10, Pisogne; 0364 87727 🚌 Regular bus service from Pisogne

MONTE ISOLA AND LAKE ISEO'S EASTERN SHORE

The eastern lake shore is dominated by Monte Isola, a traffic-free island with excellent walking. The island is accessed from Sulzano, from which a long uphill walk leads to the lovely 15th-century church of Santa Maria del Giogo. The next village is Sala Marasino, where the garden of Villa Martinengo includes the remains of a Roman villa among the flower beds.

You then take the winding road towards Zone and Europe's finest examples of **erosion pillars** – tall towers of glacial moraine created by uneven erosion. Some of the pillars are spectacularly high and some, in a surreal touch, are topped by huge boulders that originally lay on the moraine's surface. On the eastern shore, the final village is Pisogne, where the church, Santa Maria della Neve, has been called the 'Poor Man's Sistine Chapel' for the quality of the frescoes by Romanino.

✚ 138 C2

Erosion Pillars

✉ Zone, along a narrow, twisting road from Marone

Index

Acknowledgements

The Automobile Association would like to thank the following photographers, companies and picture libraries for their assistance in the preparation of this book.

Abbreviations for the picture credits are as follows – (t) top; (b) bottom; (c) centre; (l) left; (r) right; (AA) AA World Travel Library.

4l Road along Lago di Garda AA/A Mockford & N Bonetti; **4c** Scaligeri castle, Sirmione AA/A Mockford & N Bonetti; **4r** Bellagio AA/A Mockford & N Bonetti; **5l** Villa Balbianello, Lago di Como AA/A Mockford & N Bonetti; **5c** Malcesine AA/M Jourdan; **6/7** Road along Lago di Garda AA/A Mockford & N Bonetti; **10** Carnival AA/M Miterdiri; **14** Ferry times AA/A Mockford & N Bonetti; **17** Sign AA/T Harris; **20/21** Scaligeri castle, Sirmione AA/A Mockford & N Bonetti; **22/23** Bellagio AA/M Jourdan; **23br** Bellagio AA/M Jourdan; **24/25** Duomo, Milan AA/M Jourdan; **25tl** Piazza Duomo AA/M Jourdan; **26tl** Isola Bella AA/M Jourdan; **26/27** Gardens AA/M Jourdan; **27br** Isola Bella AA/C Sawyer; **28** Piazza Bra AA/C Sawyer; **28/29t** Piazza Bra AA/A Mockford & N Bonetti; **30tl** Balcony AA/M Jourdan; **30/31** Orta San Giulio AA/M Jourdan; **32bl** Contarini fountain AA/M Jourdan; **32/33** Piazza Vecchia AA/T Souter; **34/35** Santa Caterina del Sasso AA/P Bennett; **36** Castle AA/A Mockford & N Bonetti; **37** Grotte di Catullo AA/A Mockford & N Bonetti; **38bl** Sanctuary AA/A Mockford & N Bonetti; **38/39** View from Tignale road AA/A Mockford & N Bonetti; **40** Gardens AA/A Mockford & N Bonetti; **41** Cupid and Venus AA/A Mockford & N Bonetti; **42/43** Bellagio AA/A Mockford & N Bonetti; **45** La Scala AA/C Sawyer; **47** Castello Sforzesco AA/M Jourdan; **48** Museum interior AA/M Jourdan; **49** Napoleon statue AA/M Jourdan; **50/51** Santa Maria delle Grazie AA/C Sawyer; **52/53** Galleria Vittorio Emanuele AA/C Sawyer; **55** Palazzo della Ragione AA/M Jourdan; **56** Orta San Giulio AA/M Jourdan; **57** Lago di Varese AA/A Mockford & N Bonetti; **58/59** Casino Saturno Dona'/Alamy; **60/61** Morcote Marka © Michele Bella; **62bl** Castiglione Olona AA/A Mockford & N Bonetti; **62/63** Varese AA/M Jourdan; **64/65** Lugano AA/A Mockford & N Bonetti; **67** Swissminiatur AA/A Baker; **68/69** Angera AA/A Mockford & N Bonetti; **70** Fresco, Arona AA/M Jourdan; **72/73** Isola dei Pescatori AA/C Sawyer; **74/75** Castelli di Cannero AA/A Mockford & N Bonetti; **75c** Portrait of the Miracle AA/P Bennett; **76/77** Laveno AA/P Bennett; **78bl** Villa Taranto AA/P Bennett; **78/79** Pallanza AA/A Mockford & N Bonetti; **80/81** Lago Maggiore AA/A Mockford & N Bonetti; **81tr** Isola Bella AA/A Mockford & N Bonetti; **82/83** Madonna del Sasso AA/A Baker; **84/85** Basilica di San Giulio AA/M Jourdan; **86/87** Omegna Marka © Walter Zerla; **88** Villa Carlotta AA/A Mockford & N Bonetti; **89** Menaggio AA/A Mockford & N Bonetti; **91** Bellano abbey cloisters AA/M Jourdan; **92/93** Villa Maria, Cadenabbia AA/A Mockford & N Bonetti; **94/95** Duomo AA/M Jourdan; **97** Basilica di San Fedele AA/M Jourdan; **98/99** Gravedona APT del Comasco; **100/101** Lecco AA/M Jourdan; **101tr** Fishing Nets AA/A Mockford & N Bonetti; **102/103** Menaggio AA/A Mockford & N Bonetti; **104/105** Varenna AA/M Jourdan; **106/107** Colleoni chapel AA/M Jourdan; **108/109** San Pellegrino Terme AA/P Bennett; **110** Malcesine AA/A Mockford & N Bonetti; **111** Lago d'Idro AA/A Mockford & N Bonetti; **112/113** The Broletto and Torre del Popolo AA/A Mockford & N Bonetti; **114/115** Museo della Citta AA/A Mockford & N Bonetti; **116/117** Desenzano del Garda AA/M Jourdan; **118** Lago di Garda AA/A Mockford & N Bonetti; **119** Scaligeri castle AA/A Mockford & N Bonetti; **120/121** Limone sul Garda AA/M Jourdan; **121tr** Castle, Malcesine AA/A Mockford & N Bonetti; **122/123** Riva del Garda AA/M Jourdan; **124** Salo AA/A Mockford & N Bonetti; **126** Lago d'Iseo AA/M Jourdan; **127** Lago d'Iseo AA/M Jourdan; **128/129** Monte Isola AA/M Jourdan

Every effort has been made to trace the copyright holders, and we apologise in advance for any accidental errors. We would be happy to apply the corrections in the following edition of this publication.

Maps

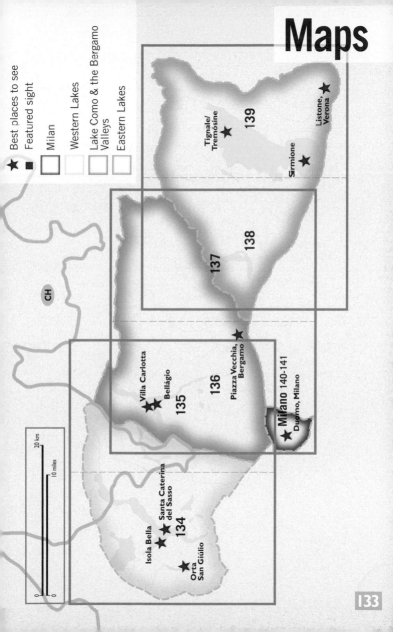

Best places to see
★ Featured sight

☐ Milan
☐ Western Lakes
☐ Lake Como & the Bergamo Valleys
☐ Eastern Lakes

CH

★ Tignale/Tremósine
139
★ Listone, Verona
★ Sirmione

137
138

★ Villa Carlotta
Bellágio
135
★ Piazza Vecchia, Bergamo
136

Milano 140-141
★ Duomo, Milano

★ Isola Bella
★ Santa Caterina del Sasso
134
★ Orta San Giúlio

20 km
10 miles

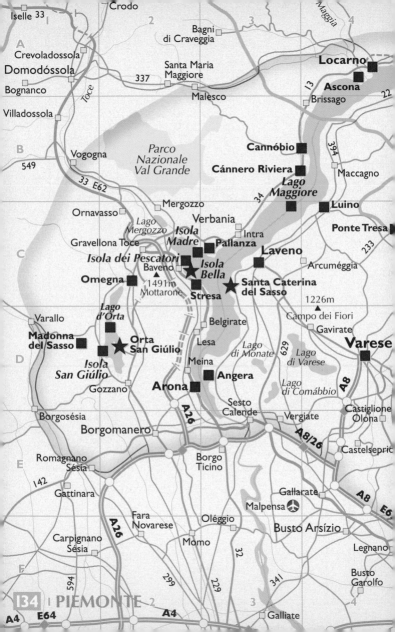

Iselle 33

Crodo

Bagni
di Craveggia

Maggia

A

Crevoladóssola

Domodóssola

Bognanco

Santa Maria
Maggiore

337

Locarno

Villadóssola

Toce

Malesco

13

Ascona

Brissago

22

B

549

Vogogna

33 E62

Ornavasso

*Parco
Nazionale
Val Grande*

Mergozzo

Cannóbio

394

Cánnero Riviera

*Lago
Maggiore*

34

Maccagno

Luino

Ponte Tresa

C

Gravellona Toce

*Lago
Mergozzo*

Verbania

Intra

233

Isola dei Pescatori

*Isola
Madre*

Baveno

Pallanza

Laveno

Arcuméggia

Omegna

▲
1491m
Mottarone

★ *Isola
Bella*

Stresa

★ **Santa Caterina
del Sasso**

1226m
▲

Campo dei Fiori

D

Varallo

*Lago
d'Orta*

Belgirate

Gavirate

629

**Madonna
del Sasso**

★ **Orta
San Giúlio**

Lesa

*Lago
di Monate*

*Lago
di Varese*

Varese

*Isola
San Giúlio*

Meina

*Lago
di Comábbio*

Gozzano

Arona

Angera

A8

Borgosésia

A26

Sesto
Calende

Vergiate

Castiglione
Olona

Borgomanero

A8/26

Castelsepric

E

Romagnano
Sésia

Borgo
Ticino

A8 E6

142

Gattinara

Gallarate

A26

Fara
Novarese

Oléggio

Malpensa ✈

Busto Arsízio

Carpignano
Sésia

Momo

32

Legnano

F

594

299

229

341

Busto
Garolfo

A4 E64

A4

Galliate

3

4

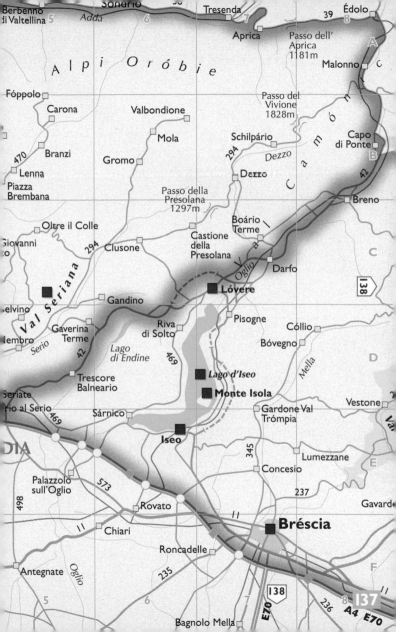

Carona
Valbondione
2 137
Vivione
1828m 3
4
Mola
Schilpário
Capo
di Ponte
Parco
delle
Rupes
Branzi
Gromo
Dezzo
294
42
Dezzo
Passo della
Presolana
1297m
Boário
Terme
Breno
Oltre il Colle
294
Clusone
Castione
della
Presolana
Darfo
Lóvere
Gandino
Pisogne
Cóllio
Gaverina
Terme
Riva
di Solto
469
Bóvegno
Lago
di Endine
Lago d'Iseo
Mella
Trescore
Balneario
Monte Isola
Vestone
237
137
Sárnico
Gardone Val
Trómpia
Val Sabbia
Iseo
345
Palazzolo
sull'Oglio
573
Lumezzane
Concesio
237
Rovato
Bréscia
Gavardo
Chiari
Roncadelle
Oglio
235
tegnate
A21 E70
A4 E70
Lon
Soncino
Orzinuovi
Bagnolo Mella
Montichiari
498
45bis
Ghedi
Castiglione
delle Stiviere
Manérbio
Leno
Carpenédolo
Verolanuova
Mella
1
2
3
4

A
B
C
D
E
F

Val Seriana
Serio
42
Oglio
Oglio
236
11
11
11

138

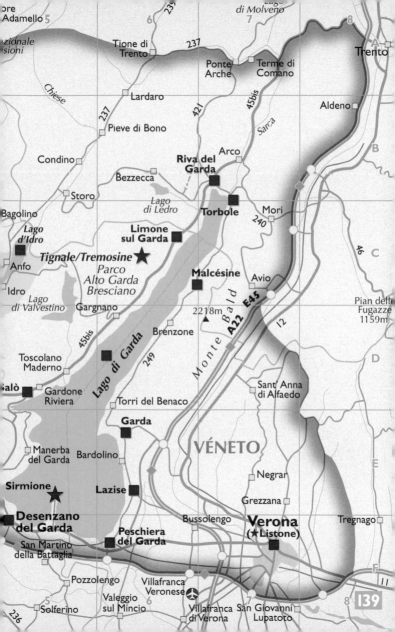

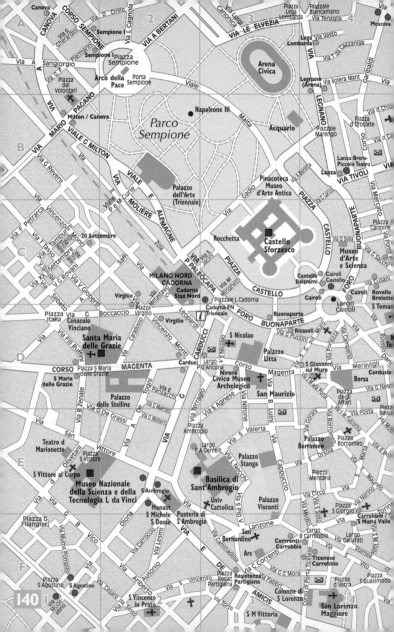

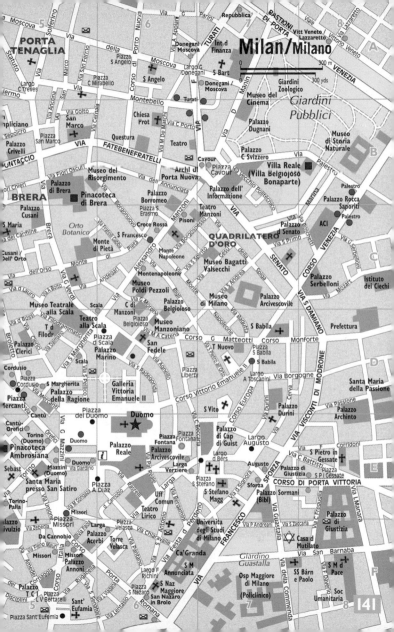

Milan/Milano

PORTA TENAGLIA

PORTA VENEZIA

Giardini Pubblici

BRERA

QUADRILATERO D'ORO

Moscova

Vitt Veneto / Lazzaretto

Int d Finanza

S Bart

Donegani / Moscova

Turati

Museo del Cinema

Giardini Zoologici

Museo di Storia Naturale

Palazzo Dugnani

Chiesa Prot

Teatro

Questura

Museo del Risorgimento

Palazzo di Brera

Pinacoteca di Brera

Archi d' Porta Nuova

Piazza Cavour

Palazzo C Svizzero

Villa Reale (Villa Belgiojoso Bonaparte)

Palazzo Rocca Saporiti

Palestro

ACI

Palazzo Serbelloni

Istituto dei Ciechi

Palazzo Crivelli

Palazzo Cusani

S Maria del Carmine

Orto Botanico

Monte di Pietà

S Francesco

Croce Rossa

Palazzo Borromeo

Teatro Manzoni

Pisoni

Palazzo dell'Informazione

Palazzo Senato

Monte Napoleone

Museo Bagatti Valsecchi

Museo Poldi Pezzoli

Montenapoleone

Museo di Milano

Palazzo Arcivescovile

Museo Teatrale alla Scala

Teatro alla Scala

Scala

Palazzo Belgiojoso

Museo Manzoniano

S Babila

Prefettura

Santa Maria della Passione

Palazzo Clerici

Teatro Filodrammatici

Palazzo Marino

San Fedele

Piazza S d Scala

T Nuovo

S Babila

Corso Monforte

Palazzo Archinto

Cordusio

Piazza Cordusio

S Margherita

Galleria Vittoria Emanuele II

Piazza Liberty

Palazzo Durini

Palazzo della Ragione

Piazza Mercanti

Cantù

Corso Vittorio Emanuele II

S Vito

Corso Europa

Cantù-Orefici

Torino (Duomo)

Pinacoteca Ambrosiana

Duomo

Piazza del Duomo

Palazzo Reale

Piazza Fontana

Palazzo di Cap di Guist

Largo Augusto

Largo d'Bers

Augusto

S Pietro in Gessate

S P i Gessate

Corridoni

Sebast

Mazzini (Duomo)

Santa Maria presso San Satiro

Duomo

Piazza A Diaz

Larga

Palazzo Arcivescovile

Larga Verziere

Piazza S Stefano

Palazzo di Giustizia

CORSO DI PORTA VITTORIA

Torino-Palla

Missori

Piazza Missori

Teatro Lirico

Uff Comun

S Stefano Magg

Palazzo Sormani (Bibl)

Palazzo di Giustizia

Cannobio

Piazza Missori

Palazzo Acerbi

Torre Velasca

Larga

Università degli Studi di Milano

Sforza

Casa d Mutilato

Piazza S Zaccaria

Missori

Palazzo Annoni

Ca'Granda

S M Annunciata

S Naz Maggiore San Nazaro in Brolo

Giardino Guastalla

Osp Maggiore di Milano (Policlinico)

SS Bárn e Paolo

S M d Pace

Sant' Eufemia

Piazza S Nazaro

Soc Umanitaria

Piazza Sant'Eufemia

300 m

300 yds

141

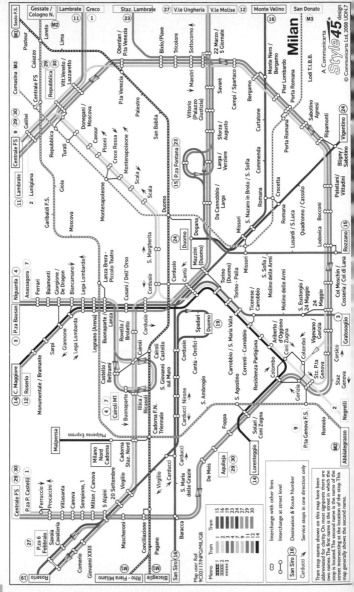

Milan

142

Notes

Titles in the series

Algarve
Amsterdam
Andalucia
Athens
Australia
Austria
Barbados
Barcelona
Brittany
Budapest
California
Canada East
Canada West
China
Corfu
Costa Blanca
Costa Brava
Costa del Sol
Crete
Croatia
Cuba
Cyprus
Disneyland Resort Paris
Dominican Republic
Dubai
Dublin
Edinburgh
Egypt
England
Florence & Tuscany
Florida
French Riviera

Gran Canaria
Ibiza & Formentera
Iceland
Ireland
Italian Lakes
Italy
Lanzarote & Fuerteventura
London
Madeira
Madrid
Mallorca
Malta & Gozo
Menorca
Mexico
Naples & the Amalfi Coast
New York
New Zealand
Normandy
Orlando
Paris
Portugal
Prague
Provence & Cote d'Azur
Rhodes
Rome
Scotland
South Africa
Tenerife
Thailand
Tunisia
Venice